THE FIRST SIXTY YEARS

THE FIRST SIXTY YEARS

1913-1973

ARTHUR ANDERSEN & CO.

PRINTED IN THE
UNITED STATES OF AMERICA

FOREWORD

In 1963, a history of Arthur Andersen & Co. was written to commemorate the fiftieth anniversary of the founding of the firm, and it was called *The First Fifty Years*. The succeeding ten years have continued to be eventful and, since it seemed desirable for each member of our organization to have an understanding of the background of such developments, it was decided that the history should be updated in a new book entitled *The First Sixty Years*. The first portion of the original history encompassing the period from December 1, 1913, through World War II has been included almost verbatim, but the sweep of history from World War II to 1973 constituted an unbroken flow of events that needed to be treated as a whole rather than being divided into smaller time segments. Essentially all of the material relating to the period from World War II to 1963 has been included in the new volume but it has been merged with the record of the last ten years.

During the sixty years since its founding, the firm has intimately touched the lives of thousands of individuals and their families who have been an integral part of Arthur Andersen & Co. This history of the firm is, in reality, a record of the combined achievements of all of these people although only a few could be named individually in the pages of this book, with its limitations of time and space.

It is hoped that all of those now living who have helped to make this history will find a sense of satisfaction and personal pride from its telling, and that it will be a source of inspiration to those now active in the firm and to all who will follow them.

ACKNOWLEDGMENTS

The First Fifty Years, which was written in 1963 and much of which has been incorporated in this book, was a cooperative effort of many people under the general direction of John A. Higgins. Chapter drafts were written by William H. Brakman, Garrett T. Burns, George R. Catlett, Grant Chandler, John A. Higgins, Wayne E. O'Quinn and Paul D. Williams. Some of the material was contributed by Walter H. Andersen and John Jirgal. Beatrice Olsen, Ida Hadley and Mildred Baker Heskett rendered valuable assistance in organizing the material in the early files. Many others helped in various ways. The final editing was done by John A. Higgins, Charles W. Jones and Paul D. Williams.

The updating and revision of the material to incorporate the events of the past ten years was completed by Mark Littler with the assistance of a number of others in the organization, including especially Carl J. Bohne, Jr., George R. Catlett, Donald M. Gamet, Joseph S. Glickauf, Jr., William J. Mueller and Claude W. Rodgers, who reviewed individual chapter drafts; Charles R. Jewell and Mildred Baker Heskett who helped immeasurably in supplying material from our files; Albert J. Bows, Jr., James A. Campbell and Paul D. Williams who served as an editorial board in reviewing the final drafts; and Charles E. Beall and the staff of our publications department (particularly John Hunsaker as design consultant) who provided continuing research assistance and support and who coordinated the multitudinous details involved in preparing the material for printing and publication.

TABLE OF CONTENTS

CONTENTS

CONTENTS

ILLUSTRATIONS

CHAPTER ONE

A Firm is Born and Starts to Grow

(1913-1920)

On December 1, 1913, Arthur Andersen founded the firm which was to bear his name and which today, sixty years later, is known throughout the world. A large measure of the success enjoyed by the firm has been due to the vision, courage, integrity and leadership of the founder and to the high standards which he set from the very beginning in determining the policies of the firm.

Clarence W. Knisely, the manager and owner of The Audit Company of Illinois, died early in November, 1913, and the net assets of this practice were acquired by Mr. Andersen and his partner, Clarence M. DeLany, from Mr. Knisely's estate. The sum of $4,000 was paid for the goodwill.

Although only 28, Mr. Andersen had already developed an extensive accounting background. Orphaned at the age of 16, he had started work as a mail boy for Fraser & Chalmers Company on the west side of Chicago where his father had been a foreman in the foundry department. This company later became a part of Allis-Chalmers Manufacturing Company. With financial help from Mr. William J. Chalmers, he managed to get

1

through high school by working during the day and going to school at night. By the time he was 21, when he married Emma Barnes Arnold, he had advanced in the Allis-Chalmers organization to the position of assistant to the controller.

One of his duties was to assist the auditors, and he found himself greatly interested in the work involved in public accounting. Job security and a fairly good salary were not enough to stifle the urge to get into public accounting and the year 1907 found him working on the Chicago staff of Price Waterhouse & Co.

A year later, Mr. Andersen passed the C.P.A. examination to become the youngest C.P.A. in Illinois at that time. In the same year, he enrolled as an evening student at the newly organized School of Commerce of Northwestern University and in the following year he was asked to teach some of the classes.

In 1911, Mr. Andersen left public accounting to become controller of Jos. Schlitz Brewing Company in Milwaukee, but he continued to commute to Chicago to teach his evening classes. The following year, the head of the accounting department at Northwestern University, Seymour Walton, resigned to found his own school of accounting, and the University invited Mr. Andersen to the position of Assistant Professor and Head of the Accounting Department, a post which he accepted. But he had been bitten by the public accounting bug, never to recover; when The Audit Company of Illinois became available in November, 1913, Mr. Andersen decided that here was the opportunity he was looking for, and on December 1, 1913, he and Mr. Delany opened their office in Chicago.

Mr. Andersen was to continue to teach at Northwestern until 1922, when he found it necessary to devote full time to his growing professional practice.

The new partnership of Andersen, DeLany & Co. issued the following announcement under date of December 1, 1913:

ANDERSEN, DeLANY & CO.
CERTIFIED PUBLIC ACCOUNTANTS

THE AUDIT COMPANY OF ILLINOIS
PUBLIC ACCOUNTANTS

A. E. ANDERSEN, C. P. A.

C. M. DELANY, C. P. A

TELEPHONE CENTRAL 5935
111 WEST MONROE ST.
(HARRIS TRUST BUILDING)
CHICAGO

ANNOUNCEMENT

ARTHUR E. ANDERSEN, PROFESSOR OF ACCOUNTING,
NORTHWESTERN UNIVERSITY, SCHOOL OF COMMERCE,

AND

CLARENCE M. DELANY,

WHO WERE FORMERLY ASSOCIATED WITH PRICE, WATERHOUSE & CO.,
DESIRE TO ANNOUNCE THAT THEY WILL ENGAGE IN THE GENERAL PRACTICE
OF PUBLIC ACCOUNTING, EMBRACING:

PERIODICAL AUDITS, INCLUDING THE PREPARATION OF BALANCE
SHEETS AND STATEMENTS OF PROFITS AND AN ANALYSIS AND
INTERPRETATION THEREOF.

THE CERTIFICATION OF FINANCIAL STATEMENTS FOR PUBLICA-
TION OR FOR PRESENTATION TO BANKERS IN SUPPORT OF APPLI-
CATIONS FOR LOANS.

INVESTIGATIONS FOR SPECIAL PURPOSES, SUCH AS TO DETERMINE
THE ADVISABILITY OF INVESTMENT IN A NEW ENTERPRISE OR
THE EXTENSION OF AN OLD BUSINESS.

THE DESIGNING AND INSTALLING OF NEW SYSTEMS OF FINANCIAL
AND COST ACCOUNTING AND ORGANIZATION, OR THE MODERN-
IZING OF EXISTING SYSTEMS.

THE PREPARATION OF REPORTS UNDER THE FEDERAL INCOME
TAX LAW.

THEY ALSO ANNOUNCE THAT THEY WILL CONTINUE THE BUSINESS OF
THE AUDIT COMPANY OF ILLINOIS, AND PRACTICE UNDER THE FIRM NAME OF

ANDERSEN, DeLANY & COMPANY
CERTIFIED PUBLIC ACCOUNTANTS

WITH OFFICES IN THE HARRIS TRUST BUILDING, CHICAGO.

DECEMBER 1, 1913.

The original office was located in Rooms 2002 and 2003 of the Harris Trust Building, 111 West Monroe Street, Chicago. The floor space aggregated 976 square feet; the annual rental was $2,100.

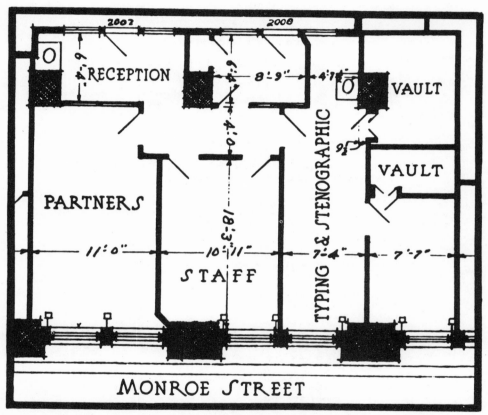

Plat of the Original Office of the Firm in Chicago

The two partners inherited all the staff from The Audit Company of Illinois. It consisted of three seniors, two semi-seniors, two juniors, and a man who kept the books and did the typing and stenographic work. The payroll for the half month's operation of the new firm (December 1-15, 1913) was as follows:

Staff	$530.09
Office	96.75
Partners' drawings	297.00
Total	$923.84

Fees billed for the month of December, 1913, aggregated $1,039.50. The largest amount billed to any one client was $614.50 to the Jos. Schlitz Brewing Company which became one of his first new clients. Today, sixty years later, the Jos. Schlitz Brewing Company is still a much valued and important client of the firm.

Fees billed by Andersen, DeLany & Co. for the first three calendar years of operation were approximately $45,400 in 1914, $54,200 in 1915 and $67,700 in 1916.

In 1918, Mr. DeLany resigned and the name of the firm was changed to Arthur Andersen & Co.

SOME EARLY CASES

During the early years of the operation of the firm, there were a number of cases which served to indicate what its policies could be expected to be under trying circumstances. Several of these cases are discussed briefly below.

About 1915, Mr. Andersen was confronted with a difficult situation with respect to the financial statements of a midwestern interurban railway company. The company had distorted its earnings by deferring relatively large charges that properly should have been absorbed in current operating expenses. Mr. Andersen was insistent that the financial statements to which he attached his report should disclose the facts. The president of the company, an autocratic man, accustomed to having his own way, came to Chicago and demanded that Mr. Andersen issue a report approving the

5

company's procedure in deferring these operating charges. Mr. Andersen informed the president that there was not enough money in the city of Chicago to induce him to change his report. We lost the client, of course, at a time when the small firm was not having easy sailing, and the loss of a client was almost a life and death matter. The soundness of Mr. Andersen's judgment in this case was clearly indicated when, a few months later, the company was forced to file a petition in bankruptcy.

The case of a Great Lakes steamship company in 1915 is of particular interest, since the decision in this case hinged on the question of the necessity of reflecting a loss which occurred after the date of the financial statements. This small steamship company had a half dozen ships rendering passenger and freight service on the Great Lakes. One of its ships, a fine new freighter, was lost in a storm early in February, 1915.

The steamship company had a bond issue coming due in 1915, and wished to use December 31, 1914, financial statements to sell refunding bonds. Since the freighter was lost in February, 1915, the company and its underwriters wished the financial statements to reflect only the situation as it actually existed at December 31, 1914. Mr. Andersen refused; he took the position that it would be misleading to issue a balance sheet that failed to recognize an important loss which had occurred after the date of the balance sheet but before the date of the refunding operation in connection with which the financial statements were to be used.

Today it is universally recognized that financial statements must give adequate recognition to material losses occurring after the date of the statements but before the date of the certificate. At that time, however, in taking this position, Mr. Andersen was blazing a new trail in the standards of financial statement presentation.

In late 1920 and the spring of 1921, there was a sharp but short-lived depression. Inventories had been accumulated far in excess of production requirements, and the losses caused by the reduction of these inventories to normal size constituted the principal characteristic of the depression. The decline in the prices of raw materials and merchandise started in the late months of 1920 and continued into the early months of 1921.

A question arose as to the proper basis of pricing the December 31, 1920, inventories. A large national public accounting firm took the position that, for financial statement purposes, inventories should be valued at the prices prevailing at December 31, 1920. Mr. Andersen disagreed with this basis of pricing; he considered that inventories should be valued on the basis of the lower price levels prevailing at the date the financial statements were issued. The business community agreed with Mr. Andersen. This concept of the proper basis of pricing is generally accepted today; in fact, it has been extended to apply to commitments for the purchase of materials or merchandise which had been entered into prior to the date of the financial statements.

Another case is of particular interest, since it was in connection with this situation that Mr. Andersen enunciated a principle which, twenty years later, gained the complete acceptance of the financial community. A prominent industrialist was arguing against Mr. Andersen's desire to correct the presentation of the industrialist's financial statements. He told Mr. Andersen that the financial statements were the company's and that there was nothing that we could do about them. Mr. Andersen agreed that the statements were the company's, but stated that the certificate issued in connection with those financial statements was ours and that he intended to determine exactly what was said in our certificate.

These cases were all very trying at the time they occurred, but a pattern began to emerge from the decisions made in these early cases that was to determine the policies and stature of the new firm.

In the fall of 1917, the firm issued a pamphlet entitled, *The Accounting Treatment of Overhead Construction Costs in Public Utilities*. This pamphlet probably represented the first serious attempt by a public accounting firm to designate the proper costs of public utility construction work and to differentiate between overhead and direct costs of construction. It also served as a useful guide for the determination of charges that could properly be capitalized by a public utility.

THE IMPACT OF THE
FEDERAL INCOME TAX LAW

The first Federal income tax, as we know it today, became effective March 1, 1913. The tax rates were so low that they had comparatively little effect upon the income of individuals or corporations. However, with the entrance of the United States into the First World War, all was changed. Income tax rates on individuals and corporations were sharply increased and an excess-profits tax on the income of corporations was enacted.

Arthur Andersen realized early the tremendous impact of these new tax laws upon individuals, corporations and the practice of public accounting. During the academic year 1917-18, the Northwestern University School of Commerce offered a special course of six lectures on Federal taxes, which was organized and given by Arthur Andersen. His brother, Walter H. Andersen, helped in the preparation of this course. The enrollment in the course was large and it included prominent judges, bankers, accountants, lawyers and business executives. Mr. Andersen's announcement of the course forecast the important influence that Federal taxes would have upon the lives of individuals and upon the national economy. The announcement read, in part, as follows:

> *"American business will be called upon to pay unusually heavy taxes during the period of reconstruction, and, therefore, a thorough knowledge of the laws and Treasury Department regulations is essential to those who are charged with the responsibility of preparing returns for individuals, partnerships, corporations and estates."*

The preparation of individual and corporate tax returns and the representation of individuals and corporations before the Treasury Department with respect to tax matters opened up wide vistas of helpful and profitable service to the public accounting profession. Very early, the firm became favorably known in the income tax field through the tax courses Mr. Andersen had given at Northwestern University, and the competent service rendered by his firm in all types of Federal tax matters under the able leadership of Walter H. Andersen and Abraham Silvertrust. Our tax work for new clients often led to other engagements in the fields of auditing, systems work and business counseling. No small part of the increase in our fees to $188,000 in 1919 and $322,000 in 1920 was due to our early preparation and vigorous effort in the field of Federal taxes.

NEW OFFICES AND NEW CLIENTS

The firm opened an office in the city of Milwaukee on October 1, 1915, with W. B. Castenholz as resident manager, followed in 1917 by Frank C. White. Andrew Peterson, who joined our Chicago office in 1922, succeeded Mr. White as resident manager in 1924. Except for a brief interlude in Chicago, Mr. Peterson was in charge of the Milwaukee office until 1950, a period of twenty-six years.

The Audit Company of Illinois had specialized to a considerable extent in work for public utility companies. A good nucleus of this work, including Consumers Power Company and Louisville Gas and Electric Company, was inherited by the new firm. Iowa Electric Light and Power Company became a client in 1915, Southern Indiana Gas and Electric Co., in 1918 and International Telephone and Telegraph Corporation, in 1920. Commercial clients acquired during the years 1913-1920 included Bergstrom Paper Company, Briggs & Stratton Corporation, Colgate-Palmolive Company, Ozite Corporation (formerly American Hair and Felt Company), The Parker Pen Company, Jos. Schlitz Brewing Company and Weyenberg Shoe Manufacturing Company. All of these companies have been clients of the firm right down to the present time.

EARLY ASSOCIATES OF ARTHUR ANDERSEN

Grant Chandler

This chapter would be incomplete if it failed to mention a few of the men who became associated with the firm during the years 1913-1920, and subsequently played an important part in the operation and development of the firm.

Grant Chandler was the first staff-man hired by Arthur Andersen. He joined the Chicago office on December 23, 1913, just twenty-two days after the firm was founded. He spent five years with the Wisconsin Railroad Commission from 1917 to 1922, and then returned to the Chicago office as office manager. Although he did an excellent job in this position, his technical ability was too valuable to permit him to be kept long in the office manager function, and he became an audit manager within a year. In this capacity, and later as a partner, Mr. Chandler specialized in public utility and Securities and Exchange Commission matters until his partial retirement in 1950. For several years thereafter, he rendered service far beyond the call of duty in reviewing audit reports and giving counsel on technical matters in many of our offices.

Charles W. Jones came to work for the firm as a junior accountant on November 1, 1914. During succeeding years, he gained a broad experience in all types of commercial and public utility accounting and auditing. He became widely known throughout the firm for his brilliant mind and for his uncanny ability to see through to the heart of an accounting problem and come up with the right answer. He was made a partner in 1924. In 1925, he transferred to New York to take charge of that office, and in 1932, he returned to Chicago and was placed in charge of our Chicago office. Mr. Jones was president of the Illinois Society of Certified Public Accountants in 1934-1935. He continued as head of the Chicago office until 1945, when he was made responsible for the important work of coordinating the auditing procedures and promulgating the accounting policies which were to be followed throughout the firm. His title was chairman of the Committee on Accounting Principles and Auditing Procedures, and he continued to function in this position with distinction until shortly before his retirement in 1959. Throughout his career, both Arthur Andersen and his successor, Leonard Spacek, relied heavily on his judgment in all matters of importance, both technical and administrative.

William C. Reyer had established a reputation in public utility circles as the chief accountant of the Wisconsin Railroad Commission. On October 1, 1915, he joined our organization and was placed in charge of our public utility practice. When the New York office of the firm was opened on June 1, 1921, Mr. Reyer was sent to New York to take charge of that office and to supervise its public utility work, which increased rapidly under his able direction. After 1925, when Charles W. Jones was transferred to the New York office, Mr. Reyer was able to devote his entire time and energy to the public utility work of that office until his untimely accidental death on May 15, 1932. Mr. Reyer was widely known as an authority on public utility accounting and finance.

Walter H. Andersen, a younger brother of Arthur Andersen, joined our organization in the fall of 1916. Although he specialized on problems encountered in connection with Federal taxes and financial investigations, he was thoroughly versed in all branches of commercial auditing and accounting. He was in charge of the Chicago office of the firm from 1919 until his resignation in 1932. He possessed a very kindly and understanding nature and was gifted with extraordinary intellectual capacity. His advice on accounting, financial and Federal tax problems was often sought by Chicago bankers, underwriters, lawyers and businessmen, and he had an important part in the early growth of the firm. He was president of the Illinois Society of Certified Public Accountants in the year 1931-1932.

Paul K. Knight joined the organization on October 8, 1917. His progress was rapid. Four years later he was one of the top commercial managers in the Chicago office, and when the Kansas City office was opened on November 1, 1923, he was transferred to Kansas City and placed in charge of that office. He was made a partner on July 1, 1925, and was transferred to the New York office in the fall of that year. When Mr. Jones was brought back to Chicago in 1932, Paul Knight was placed in charge of the New York office. He filled this position with distinction until 1950, when he became an advisory partner in the New York office. He continued to function in this capacity until his death on August 24, 1957. Mr. Knight was known throughout the firm for his urbanity, his humor, his remarkable administrative ability, and for his extraordinary common sense which enabled him, time and again, to come up with the simple, practical answer to a complicated technical question or business problem.

John Jirgal came with the firm in 1920, with a background of broad experience in the public utility field. He was in charge of the public utility work of the Chicago office from 1921 until 1932, when he became responsible for the supervision of the public utility work in all offices of the firm. He continued in this capacity until his resignation from the firm in 1938. Mr. Jirgal played a major role in the Insull engagement, which is discussed in Chapter Three.

CHAPTER TWO

Expansion in the Twenties

The firm was becoming better known outside the midwest area as the result of the unusual techniques it developed in making financial and business investigations. This was a period of expansion in industry, rapid growth of individual companies and mergers of small companies into larger, integrated units. Much of this expansion was financed by bond or preferred stock issues. Investment bankers, principally in New York and Chicago, were very active in promoting financing business for themselves by taking the initiative in encouraging expansion and mergers. Their main problem was to distinguish between the good risks and the bad risks.

This was a major source of new work for us, since we had developed the manpower, the competence and the methods for obtaining and presenting the information the banker needed in order to decide whether or not to go through with the financing arrangements under consideration. In many cases, the investment banker was our client.

FINANCIAL INVESTIGATIONS

The firm developed financial investigation reports which went into many phases of a business other than financial and accounting, including labor relations, availability of raw materials, plants, products, markets, effectiveness of the organization and future prospects. The methods which were used in developing these reports involved a study of company policies and their effectiveness, and the performance of management in carrying them out.

Reports on financial and business investigations were presented in considerable detail, with a summary of our findings and recommendations in the first section. The reports usually contained financial statements for a period of several years, and often included summaries of sales, earnings, dividends and changes in surplus from the inception of the business. Based upon these investigations, we made recommendations looking toward accounting and operating improvements and commented on the outlook for profitable operations. These reports were used by investment bankers and others preliminary to financing the enterprises, and in many instances were used by the managements of the companies for the purpose of considering and implementing our recommendations.

The risks in this type of work were considerable, but the results were important to a young firm, struggling to become known and established nationally, as we often became the regular auditors of the companies involved. Assignments of this nature enhanced our reputation with bankers and the business community for having the ability and courage to go rather deeply into the operations and economics of a business situation.

With the crash of 1929, financing engagements dwindled, and this type of work with its many ramifications and risks was practically discontinued in 1930. Some of the techniques developed in the financial investigation work, however, were adopted in the firm's regular auditing procedures, particularly those concerning the balance of inventory quantities of the various products with sales requirements, problems of inventory obsolescence and the pricing of inventories. The inventory procedures which had been developed were very effective in our auditing work, particularly in the postwar depression of 1921, when many companies had accumulated inventories substantially in excess of normal requirements.

ADDITIONAL OFFICES REQUIRED

The demand for our services in making financial investigations, as well as the increasing effectiveness of our work in the fields of auditing, Federal taxation, and special services to management, resulted in the rapid growth of our practice during this decade. Six additional offices were opened, in New York, Washington, Kansas City, Los Angeles, San Francisco and Detroit; and in 1930, Arthur Andersen and Charles W. Jones made arrangements in London for representation in Europe, South America and Southeast Asia as a result of our expanding work abroad.

The rapidly growing tax practice of the firm required that we have convenient access to the Internal Revenue Service, and on January 1, 1921, an office was opened in Washington, D. C., under the direction of Sebastian H. Hook. He was followed in 1923 by Walter F. Mehrlich, who later transferred to Chicago.

William C. Reyer, assisted by Edwin F. Chinlund, opened the New York office in 1921. In 1925, Charles W. Jones was transferred from Chicago to take charge of the New York office. Paul K. Knight, who had opened the Kansas City office in 1923, was also transferred to the New York office in 1925. At that time, Paul D. Williams was placed in charge of the Kansas City office. He remained there until 1933, when he was put in charge of the Detroit office on account of the illness of Frederic D. Utley, who had opened the Detroit office in 1930. The Los Angeles office was opened in 1926 by Amos L. Moreton, and the San Francisco office in 1928 by E. Arnold Sunstrom.

THE NEW YORK OFFICE

The New York office commenced operations on June 1, 1921, at 17 East 42nd Street in the midtown area. It occupied an area of only 733 square feet and consisted of five rooms.

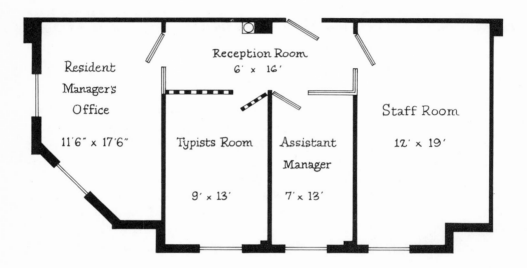

Plat of the Firm's Original New York Office on 42nd Street

As the practice developed, it became apparent that the 42nd Street location was not suitable, since most of our clients were located in downtown New York, and considerable time was lost in riding the subways between our office and the offices of our clients. In connection with our search for a downtown location, it is interesting to note that Arthur Andersen cautioned against a long-term lease, as indicated in the following excerpt from his letter dated August 15, 1924:

> *"I do not believe that we should tie ourselves up for a longer term than five years in New York. The probability is that one of two things will happen, i.e., we will require additional space, or we will have proven that there is no place for us in New York. I am quite sure, as all of us are, that the former condition is the one that is likely to prevail, but in any case it is desirable not to enter into a lease for a longer term than five years."*

Suitable space was located at 67 Wall Street and the New York office moved to that location on July 1, 1925, where it remained until 1950.

GROWTH IN PERSONNEL AND VOLUME

In 1920, the organization of the firm consisted of two partners and fifty-four employees, including managers, staff and office personnel. In 1922, the partnership was expanded to five, and by 1930, to seven. In the latter year, there was a total complement of three hundred seventy-eight, including the seven partners and twenty-nine managers. These partners, and the years in which they were admitted to the firm, were Arthur Andersen (1913), Walter H. Andersen (1922), John Jirgal (1922), William C. Reyer (1922), Frank White (1922), Charles W. Jones (1924) and Paul K. Knight (1925).

The substantial growth of the firm during the ten-year period of the 1920's is indicated by the increase in fees from approximately $322,000 in 1920 to $2,023,000 in 1929. Fees in 1930 were slightly less than in 1929. The depression following 1929 did not seriously affect the long-range growth of the firm; however, the fee level of 1929 was not reached again until 1935.

Of the total fees of $1,956,000 in 1930, the Chicago office contributed $1,078,000 and the New York office, $543,000. The fees of the Milwaukee, Kansas City, Los Angeles and San Francisco offices aggregated $335,000. During the ten-year period 1921-1930, Chicago office fees showed a significant increase of approximately $775,000. The New York office, which realized fees of $101,000 in its first full year of operation (1921-1922), increased its fees to $586,000 in 1928. This was a remarkable performance, considering the fact that the firm, based in Chicago, was practically unknown in the New York area when the office was opened, and was in competition with the large, long-established public accounting firms with headquarters in New York.

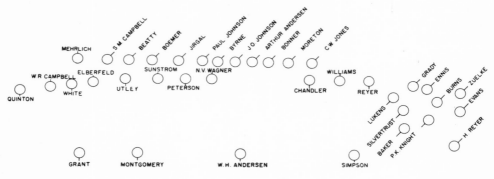

Partners' and Managers' Meeting, October 10, 1930

CHAPTER THREE

The Depression and Post-depression Years

(1931-1940)

The decade of the 1930's was a period of challenge and testing. In common with practically all professional and industrial enterprises, the firm saw its business curtailed and its profits drastically reduced during the depression years. Fees which had aggregated $2,023,000 in 1929 sank to a low of $1,488,000 in 1932. However, the firm came out of this difficult period with a national reputation for integrity, competence and constructive service.

A number of major industrial and commercial companies became clients during the depression years, and the addition of the Insull companies to our clientele gave a special impetus to our work in the regulated industry field.

THE INSULL COMPANIES

In spite of the depression of the early thirties, Samuel Insull had determined that the operating companies in his far-flung utility empire should not pursue a policy of retrenchment but should continue their normal construction and property acquisition programs. Millions of dollars were spent by the companies for new construction and for the acquisition of additional properties in 1930 and 1931, when a more conservative policy would have counseled the curtailment of such expenditures and the husbanding of cash resources. Apparently, Mr. Insull, like some other executives at the time, was acting on the belief that if companies generally would continue to expand and build, it would help to end the depression. The bonded debt of the companies in the system, already high in many instances on the basis of intrinsic underlying values, was greatly increased to finance this expansion.

Late in 1928, Mr. Insull had organized an investment trust, Insull Utilities Investment Company, and soon thereafter, a second investment trust known as Corporation Securities Company. These trusts were availed of to provide funds for the purchase of large blocks of the equity securities of the Insull system operating and holding companies. In addition to public financing, including the issuance of capital stock, the trusts borrowed heavily from the large New York and Chicago banks. The bank loans were of short term and were collateralized principally by the deposit of equity securities of the operating companies, which securities had been acquired after the public financing had been consummated. By early 1932, the securities used as collateral had declined in value to a point where they no longer adequately protected the bank loans, and the bankers became greatly concerned as to the collectibility of their loans. They, therefore, entered into a stand-still agreement under which their loans and collateral were not to be changed.

At this point, Arthur Andersen was asked to become the Chicago representative of the New York banks, and in that connection the firm made high-spot investigations in order to familiarize itself with the financial affairs of the Insull companies, with which it previously had had no relations. This information was necessary to enable Mr. Andersen to function as the representative of the bankers.

He was also asked to operate a control procedure in order to make certain that all current expenditures and financial transactions of the principal Insull companies were of such a nature as not to change or impair the collateral position of the banks. This was an unusual and difficult assignment, certainly not in the ordinary run of public accounting engagements. However, Mr. Andersen felt that, as a public duty in the acute economic situation of the country in general and the financial condition of these companies in particular, he should undertake this assignment. For a considerable period, members of our organization approved all vouchers and important financial transactions of the principal Insull companies. This approval was in addition to, and not in lieu of, the customary corporate approvals, as the firm rightfully declined to assume management responsibility.

To implement these activities and to conserve the energies of the various people involved, partners of Arthur Andersen & Co. met nearly every day in the firm's office with representatives of the Insull companies and of the Chicago bankers to pass upon transactions which might affect the stand-still agreement. The Middle West Utilities Company, the investment companies, the electric railway companies, and some of the other units were in such bad financial condition that they were forced to file petitions in receivership. However, Commonwealth Edison and its affiliated companies and The Peoples Gas Light and Coke Company, the large and important Insull units in the Chicago area, were successfully financed in 1932, and the other principal operating utility companies in the Insull system were brought through their crises and have continued as financially sound and prosperous companies to this day.

Thus, the fall of the Insull empire and the successful efforts to rehabilitate the principal operating companies in the group became a matter of financial history, and the reputation of Arthur Andersen & Co. was enhanced by this demonstration of its ability to meet a difficult and demanding situation with courage and competence. As a result of the effective manner in which the whole situation was handled, the firm was retained as auditors for almost all of the Insull companies, although by that time they were under many different managements and, in a number of instances, were under the supervision of the courts. Even more important, the firm became known and recognized favorably by the highest echelon of officers of the leading banks and financial institutions of this country.

At this time our public utility practice was under the direction of John Jirgal. He was followed by Leonard Spacek (1940-1947), F. Merrill Beatty (1947-1963) and Richard Walker (1963 to date).

SAFEGUARDING THE PURCHASER
OF SECURITIES

The collapse of the securities markets in the fall of 1929 and the extraordinary losses suffered by millions of people were due in a large measure to the speculative frenzy that had seized the American people in 1928 and 1929. This had driven up stock prices to a point where market prices did not bear the remotest relation to earning power and intrinsic values. However, there had also been a lamentable weakness in corporate reporting, and the prospectuses issued in connection with security offerings frequently failed to give a fair statement of earnings and financial condition.

The Securities Act of 1933 was enacted for the purpose of affording additional protection to purchasers of securities. Under this act, a corporation issuing securities, its officers and directors, the underwriters, and the experts who had expressed an opinion with respect to the fairness of the financial statements or the intrinsic value of its property could be held liable to make good any loss suffered by an investor who had purchased the securities in reliance upon the financial statements and the financial facts disclosed in the prospectus issued in connection with the offering, if there had been material omissions or misstatements in the prospectus.

At this time, an important change occurred with respect to the concept of an accountant's responsibility for the financial statements which he certified. Hitherto the theory had been accepted that the public accountant examined the books of account and related records and then prepared the financial statements which he certified. The new concept, which soon became universally accepted, was that the financial statements were the representations of the company. The public accountant's function was to examine these financial statements, agree with the company, if possible, on any material adjustments required, and express his opinion as to whether the statements had been prepared in accordance with generally accepted accounting principles consistently applied, and fairly presented the financial position and results of operations. Under this concept, the company has the original responsibility for the fairness of the financial statements, but in signing his certificate with respect to those statements, the public accountant places his professional opinion on the line that the statements are fair and that they reflect accepted accounting practices.

The administration of the Securities Act of 1933 and the Securities Exchange Act of 1934 has done much to raise the standards of corporate reporting in connection with security offerings. As was probably true of many of the national firms, our practice increased materially from the many cases where the firm was asked by new clients to examine their financial statements which were to be included in prospectuses issued in connection with registering their security offerings.

ORIGINAL COST OF PUBLIC
UTILITY PROPERTIES

About 1935, the concept was quite generally accepted by public utility regulatory authorities that utility properties should be carried on the books and valued for rate purposes at "original cost," which was defined as the cost when first devoted to public service. The application of this concept to utility properties made it highly desirable that the original cost of such properties be determined and that continuous unit property records be established in order to facilitate the accounting for property on the original-cost basis.

Leonard Spacek, who started his public accounting career in our Chicago office in 1928, pioneered in assisting our utility clients to establish unit property records. The installation of these records required an immense amount of detailed clerical work, which was performed by company employees under our direction. Eventually, unit property records were installed under our supervision by a large number of the utility clients of the firm. Once such records were installed, the mysteries previously associated with the accounts for "property rights, franchises, etc.," were ended for all time.

WORLD'S FAIRS

Despite the depression, a world's fair, aptly named "A Century of Progress," was held on the Chicago lake front during the years 1933 and 1934. The holding of a world's fair during such a period was positive evidence that the I WILL spirit of Chicago was still a driving force. Our firm was brought into the picture to install a system providing for the adequate control of the revenues, expenses and capital expenditures of the fair. The installation of this system was carried out under the over-all supervision of Garrett T. Burns.

In 1939-1940, a world's fair was held by the city of New York. In the meantime, Mr. Burns had been transferred to our New York office, and when our firm was requested to install a system of controls for the New York World's Fair, Mr. Burns was able to use to great advantage the experience he had gained in the development of the accounting controls for the Century of Progress in Chicago.

The fees charged by the firm for its services in connection with these two world's fairs were relatively modest. This work was undertaken as a community service, and was significant chiefly from a public interest point of view.

POST-DEPRESSION GROWTH

The post-depression years, 1934 to 1940, were a period of growth and progress for the firm. While many important new clients were added during this period, the additions to the firm's clientele were by no means confined to large companies. The mainstay of any public accounting practice is always the small and medium-sized company. Under the leadership of J. O. Johnson of the Chicago office, our service to small businesses was emphasized and substantially enlarged. Eventually, separate small business divisions were established in our various offices, in order to give better service to small companies.

Four new offices were opened by the firm during the latter part of this decade: Boston and Houston in 1937, Atlanta and Minneapolis in 1940. The Boston office was opened by Harry I. Prankard, II, and the Minneapolis office, by Wallace E. Lunden. The Houston office was opened by Joe D. Beasley and the Atlanta office by William J. Nettles.

Partners, Managers and Wives at Twenty-fifth Anniversary Dinner, 1938

CHAPTER FOUR

The War Years

(1941-1946)

The period of the Second World War introduced many new problems and challenges to the accounting profession. The requirements of the armed forces for weapons, transportation and food took precedence over civilian needs, and the nation found itself operating under a regulated economy. Because profits were limited by legislation such as the Vinson-Trammel, Merchant Marine and Renegotiation Acts, business concerns were forced to pay close attention to the accounting implications of their government contracts. They also had to take a much deeper interest in their established accounting procedures.

SPECIAL PROBLEMS OF THE WAR ECONOMY

One of the principal problems which companies and their auditors had to face during this period was the renegotiation of contract prices. As the war effort developed, Congress provided for the renegotiation of substantially all war contracts. This process enabled the government to recover any profit in excess of the profit which it determined to be appropriate.

The renegotiation process was complicated and time-consuming. The government always had the last word as to the percentage of profit allowed, but it was important that the companies involved make an effective presentation of the pertinent financial and operating facts. Many commercial companies relied on their public accountants for the preparation of their renegotiation cases and our firm did a substantial amount of work in this field. Our renegotiation work was under the general direction of Garrett T. Burns.

The drastic changes brought about by the war affected every kind of business. Manufacturing companies, faced with the tremendous requirements of war production, were often forced to expand to three or four times their previous size. New lines were added, and, in some cases, the very character of their operations was radically changed. These expansions had to be financed, and if a government agency was availed of for this purpose, new accounting and reporting procedures were prescribed.

In order to obtain certain raw materials, it was necessary to establish and maintain the right to a priority classification, and this required additional analyses and reports to government agencies. New plant facilities acquired for war production could be amortized over a five-year period for financial accounting and income-tax purposes, but the paper work involved in obtaining certificates of necessity as a basis for the five-year amortization was an added burden on the accounting department personnel. These burdens became so heavy that many small and medium-sized companies called on their public accountants for assistance in matters which would normally have been handled by company employees.

With the large increases in tax rates, the charge for income taxes became just about the most significant figure in the income statement. The concern of management over the income-tax angles of their operations caused them to seek tax counsel on a year-round basis rather than just before or after the close of the fiscal year. Tax laws and regulations were changing rapidly. Our professional staff not only had to be familiar with current laws, but also with the status of prospective changes which were being discussed in Congress. By so doing, they were able to provide a basis for management to make the best possible estimate of the tax impact on transactions which were contemplated and on the operation as a whole.

There were other problems that required constant watching by company managements and their auditors. For example, there might be excessive inventory accumulations which would cause losses due to lack of future need or postwar price declines. The same dangers existed with regard to plant facilities, as the usual depreciation rates might well be inadequate to take care of losses due to excess capacity when the war-production demands ceased. Manufacturers, however patriotic, were quite naturally reluctant to expand their inventories and plant facilities to handle business that would probably vanish or decrease materially with the passing of the national emergency, especially since income and excess-profits taxes would usually absorb from 50% to 75% of the wartime profits.

THE IMPACT OF THE WAR ON OUR FIRM

During the previous decade, the firm had established the policy of strengthening the personnel of all offices so that each office would be self-sustaining. The timing of this development was most fortunate, since it enabled us to serve our clients effectively throughout the country during this difficult period, notwithstanding the personnel losses due to enlistments, drafting of younger men and attractive salaries offered by companies engaged in war production.

On account of our severe losses of personnel, the men who remained had to work very hard in order to cover our commitments. Practically all of our offices went on a six-day-week basis. This, however, represented a minimum schedule, since overtime of a substantial amount was the general rule.

Our opportunities for service were broadened by the acquisition of certain new clients who were important to the war effort. For example, in the shipbuilding industry we had acquired as clients the Newport News Shipbuilding and Dry Dock Company and the Bath Iron Works; also the Cramp Ship Yard at Philadelphia, which was revived after many idle years. We assisted in that revival right from the beginning in connection with accounting, personnel and other matters.

Toward the end of World War II, and afterward, a new set of problems was introduced by contract terminations. Prompt reconversion to civilian production meant survival to some companies, and it was essential that termination claims be prepared and settled as expeditiously as possible. Many dollars of previously recorded costs and expected profits were frequently in jeopardy.

In order to assist our clients effectively in the preparation and processing of claims, it was necessary to gain a thorough understanding of the termination regulations and the procedures which would satisfy the government agencies involved. Our clients had to be carefully advised as to what objections might be raised to their claims, as well as what procedures would be helpful in substantiating them. Services in these areas naturally encountered more appreciation than strictly technical help. Despite many difficulties, we were able to serve our clients, preserve our independence and maintain the confidence of all of the parties involved.

Lest the impression be given that our work during the war years was limited to clients engaged solely or principally in production for war, it should be noted that we also acquired a number of important clients active in other fields. These engagements had to be properly handled, notwithstanding our personnel problems and the added burdens of wartime accounting.

One of the grave dangers inherent in a difficult situation, such as existed during the war, is a tendency to relax the old standards for the duration. Our firm was fortunate in having the leadership of partners who insisted on maintaining the same standards and principles which had guided us from the inception of the firm.

In 1944, more than 50% of our permanent staff were in the armed forces. The majority of these men were in combat units but a large number were assigned to cost inspection and other types of work which made use of their previous training. Several of our present partners served in positions which were important to the war effort, and many of them feel that their war experience was of great value to them in the development of their later careers.

During this period four new offices were opened. The St. Louis and Seattle offices were opened in 1943 by L. Wayne Lutyens and Lester E. Burmeister and in 1946, offices were opened in Cleveland by Donald J. Erickson and in Philadelphia by Marion F. Stone, making a total in 1946 of sixteen offices.

The men who joined our organization during this difficult period, 1941-1946, included one hundred fifty-five who later became partners and managers. The number of such men hired in one year reached the low point of twelve in 1944, but it increased to twenty-seven in 1945 and thirty-eight in 1946, reflecting the stepping up of our recruiting activities as the war ended.

CHAPTER FIVE

Transition in Leadership

(1947)

THE LOSS OF THE FOUNDER

Arthur Andersen had been ailing in 1946 and his death came on January 10, 1947, at the age of 61. The initial impact of losing the strong leadership of the founder of the firm was severe. A few days after his death, the twenty-five men who were his partners at that time issued the following statement:

"To All Personnel of the Firm

"The death of Mr. Arthur Andersen was a shock that was felt very, very deeply by all who have known him. The sense of keen personal loss that we all have springs from our appreciation of the substantial influence that he has been in our lives. His contribution to our welfare should never be forgotten by any person who has been or ever will be associated with this firm.

"Mr. Andersen, in building and developing the firm, anticipated the tragic event of last week and during the past few years a great deal of his time and thought was devoted to measures that

would insure the continuance of the firm on the same high level after he had gone.

"His passing came many years earlier than he or any of us thought possible, but by reason of his foresight the firm will continue to operate aggressively and will adhere to the same policies of integrity, high level of service, and opportunity for every member of our organization.

"Mr. Andersen has left us a heritage for which we shall be eternally grateful. We will show our gratitude by carrying forward with a united spirit and with the same determination of purpose that characterized his life; by doing so, the Arthur Andersen & Co. of the future can be built into something even finer than the one Mr. Andersen left us.

The Partners of the Firm"

CHOOSING A SUCCESSOR

Arthur Andersen had become an important and highly respected figure in the business world. Naturally, there was considerable concern over the nature and extent of public reaction to his loss and its effect on the future of the organization.

The firm was by no means lacking in capable men who could serve ably as managing partner, but there was no one on the horizon who approached the public stature of Arthur Andersen. The founder and first managing partner had been only twenty-eight years old when he assumed his task, but would it be wise, under all of the circumstances, to choose a relatively young man to take his place?

After much soul-searching, the question was resolved by the election of Leonard Spacek, aged thirty-nine, as managing partner of the firm and Paul K. Knight and Charles W. Jones to the policy-making positions of chairman and vice chairman of the partnership.

Mr. Spacek was already deeply involved with the firm's administration and was familiar with all phases of its operations. He had started as a junior accountant in 1928 and had worked through successive stages of professional responsibility, becoming a partner in 1940 when he was placed in charge of the firm's work in the regulated industry field. In 1945, he had become the partner in charge of the Chicago office which, at that time, contained over 30% of the total organization.

That the choice of Leonard Spacek as Mr. Andersen's successor was a sound one soon became evident. In a short time, he demonstrated his abilities as the chief executive, and the firm leaped forward under his direction. He quickly expanded the ranks of the partnership, strengthened the total management structure, improved communications within the firm and otherwise laid the groundwork for the tremendous expansion that was to follow. Three years later, in 1950, Charles W. Jones made these comments to the young men in that year's staff training school:

"In Leonard Spacek, the managing partner, this firm has a leader who, I think, is second to none. I wouldn't trade him for any two other men in the public accounting profession. He is aggressive; he has a very unusual intellect; he has an enormous capacity for work; he has an abiding interest in the firm of Arthur Andersen & Co. and in the young men composing it. This should mean a lot to every one of you men. I am positive that under his leadership the firm will continue to grow and develop. There is no sign of anything else. Many wondered after Mr. Andersen's death three years ago just what would happen. The only thing that has happened is that there has been a substantial growth of our business. That happened not because of his death, but because a tremendous effort was made by all of the partners, but particularly by Leonard Spacek, to make it happen."

CHAPTER SIX

The Era of Rapid Growth

(1947 to the Present Time)

GROWTH OF THE ECONOMY

During the period immediately following World War II, the civilian economy expanded rapidly. The pent-up demand of the war years burst upon the economic scene with explosive force. Industrial companies which had been running full steam on war production had difficulty in converting to civilian production fast enough to meet the demand. But this proved to be only the beginning of a prolonged period of expansion which, except for a few temporary setbacks, has continued to the present time, as indicated by the following chart based on statistics taken from government publications:

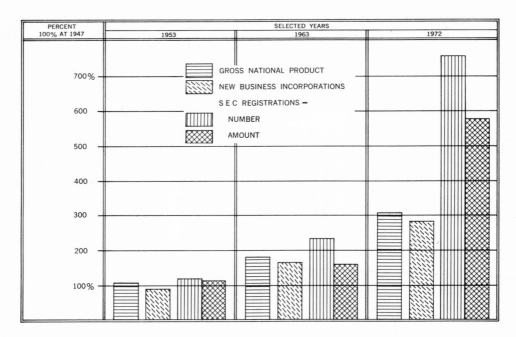

PERCENT 100% AT 1947	SELECTED YEARS		
	1953	1963	1972

GROSS NATIONAL PRODUCT
NEW BUSINESS INCORPORATIONS
S E C REGISTRATIONS —
NUMBER
AMOUNT

PARALLEL GROWTH OF OUR FIRM

Obviously, the demands on the public accounting profession during these years were enormous and a period of rapid growth was inevitable. Data are not available on the profession as a whole, but it is clear from the statistics on our firm, which follow, that our growth compares favorably with the pattern of the national economy.

	1947	1953	1963	1973
U. S. Offices—				
Chargeable hours	1,132,000	2,042,000	3,946,000	9,350,000
Total personnel	848	1,603	3,320	8,836
Number of offices	16	18	34	45
Non-U. S. Offices—				
Chargeable hours	—	—	920,000	3,308,000
Total personnel	—	—	911	3,484
Number of offices	—	—	26	47
Combined—				
Chargeable hours	1,132,000	2,042,000	4,866,000	12,658,000
Total personnel	848	1,603	4,231	12,320
Number of offices	16	18	60	92
Number of clients	2,300	6,000	19,000	50,000

Our growth in total personnel from 848 in 1947 to 12,320 in 1973 may be analyzed as follows:

Offices Opened	Personnel			
	1947	1953	1963	1973
1913-1946:				
Chicago (opened in 1913)	255	471	736	1,566
New York (opened in 1921) ...	191	291	512	884
14 other U. S. offices	402	780	1,502	3,971
	848	1,542	2,750	6,421
1947-1953:				
2 U. S. offices	—	61	123	276
1954-1963:				
16 U. S. offices	—	—	447	1,400
26 non-U. S. offices	—	—	911	2,578
	—	—	1,358	3,978
1964-1973:				
11 U. S. offices	—	—	—	739
21 non-U. S. offices (net)	—	—	—	906
	—	—	—	1,645
	848	1,603	4,231	12,320

The Chicago and New York offices grew substantially after 1947 although the ratio of their combined personnel to the total for the firm dropped from 53% in 1947 to 20% in 1973. This salutary trend toward a broader base of operations resulted from both the opening of new offices and the rapid growth of the fourteen offices, other than Chicago and New York, established prior to 1947.

The offices opened in the United States from 1947 to 1973 are shown below by the periods corresponding to the above tabulation:

U. S. Offices Opened from 1947 to 1973

1947-1953	1954-1963	1964-1973
Dallas	Birmingham	Baltimore
Omaha	Charlotte	Boise
(2)	Chattanooga	Columbus
	Cincinnati	Long Island
	Denver	Memphis
	Fort Worth	Miami
	Hartford	Rochester
	Indianapolis	San Jose
	Newark	Santa Ana
	New Orleans	Stamford
	Oklahoma City	Tampa
	Phoenix	(11)
	Pittsburgh	
	Portland	
	San Juan	
	Tulsa	
	(16)	

The growth of the firm outside of the United States during the same period was also dramatic, with the opening of 52 new offices in financial centers around the world. Our development into a worldwide organization during this period is covered at greater length in Chapter Seven.

With the increase in the number of the firm's clients from 2,300 in 1947 to 50,000 in 1973, many well-known companies were added to our client list. An interesting phenomenon accompanying this growth has been the growth in the percentage of companies listed on the New York Stock Exchange which are audited by the firm. In 1947, we audited 72 listed companies which represented 7% of all listed companies. In that year, each of five other accounting firms audited more listed companies than we did.

In 1973, by contrast, the firm audited 258 listed companies which represented 17% of all listed companies and was larger than the number audited by any other accounting firm.

SOME IMPACTS ON THE FIRM OF
THE ERA OF RAPID GROWTH

The impact of our growth over this extended period of time on every member of the organization has been tremendous. Not only has it demanded considerable personal sacrifice, but it has caused the firm, among other things, to study and revise its organization structure and operating methods from time to time, and to sharpen its communications to the end that this growth could be assimilated properly and a solid foundation built for future growth.

It was necessary to expand the partnership base rather substantially and, at the same time, to strengthen our "one-firm" concept of operations. The growing demands on our professional staff called for an acceleration in the hiring, training and development of our people and the further strengthening of our professional competence. Along with this, we felt the need to undertake an expanded leadership role in the profession as a whole.

Some of the major steps taken to accomplish these objectives are reviewed in subsequent chapters.

Partners' Meeting, 1953

Partners' Meeting, 1973

41

CHAPTER SEVEN

The Development into a Worldwide Organization

Nowhere in our history has the one-firm concept played a greater role than in the development of our operations outside of the United States. Arthur Andersen & Co. is now a worldwide organization of partners of many nationalities who adhere to the same objectives of professional leadership and client service while complying with the laws and professional ethics of the countries in which they practice. We are thus able to conduct our practice on a uniform basis throughout the world. Boston and Brussels, San Francisco and São Paulo are similarly organized and operated.

This approach to worldwide operations was not conceived without considerable experimentation and change. In the early stages, representation arrangements were established under which leading accounting firms throughout the world handled our overseas work, with provision for direct participation by our firm where required. Later, there were joint undertakings between our firm and firms in other countries, and direct supervision was exercised to a greater extent. By and large, these early arrangements were not satisfactory because of the variations in levels of service, training, and quality of work that were available in the various countries. Finally, the concept of Arthur Andersen & Co. offices, supervised and manned by Andersen-trained personnel, was adopted.

Basic to this new approach was the policy that our practice in countries outside of the United States would be built with local nationals who would be recruited from local universities and who would be offered the same training and the same opportunities for personal development and recognition in our worldwide organization as those recruited in the United States.

This was a new and revolutionary approach. In most countries outside the United States, the accounting profession traditionally had employed mostly non-college people and in many countries, opportunities to achieve partnership status in the international firms were rarely open to local nationals. Our policies in this respect proved to be sound. By the end of 1973, total personnel outside the United States had grown to almost 3,500, most of whom were local nationals. Of 826 worldwide partners and participating principals in 1973, 137 were nationals of countries other than the United States. Nationals of other countries have served as members of the Board of Directors since its inauguration in 1968. All partners and participating principals share in the same worldwide profit pool.

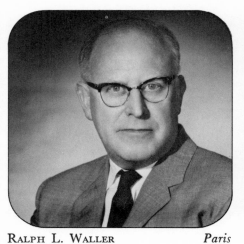

RALPH L. WALLER *Paris*
Admitted July 1, 1952

FRANK A. FORD *São Paulo*
Admitted January 1, 1958

JOHN K. LITTLE *Melbourne*
Admitted July 1, 1959

NICOLÁS URQUIZA *México City*
Admitted July 1, 1959

STEPHEN ELLIOTT *Toronto*
Admitted July 1, 1960

J. ANDRÉS RUIZ *México City*
Admitted July 1, 1960

The First Six Partners Outside the United States

The development into a worldwide organization thus was accomplished in three major phases—representation arrangements (prior to World War II), joint undertakings (end of World War II to the mid-1950's), and the establishing of our own offices (mid-1950s to the present).

PRIOR TO WORLD WAR II

It was not until after World War I that United States capital commenced to flow abroad in any appreciable amount. As early as 1926, the firm, then only thirteen years old, was giving serious consideration to means of serving the overseas operations of its clients.

In 1930, Arthur Andersen and Charles W. Jones visited London and made arrangements with McAuliffe, Davis & Hope to represent Arthur Andersen & Co. in Europe, South America and the Far East. This firm merged with Turquand, Youngs & Co. in 1938 to form McAuliffe, Turquand, Youngs & Co. with the McAuliffe name later being dropped.

In those early years, the firm's clients with operations in Europe included Associated Telephone and Telegraph Company, International Telephone and Telegraph Corporation, Colgate-Palmolive Company, and The Texas Company (now Texaco, Inc.). Since most of the European work was for New York-based clients, the liaison between the two firms was centered in the New York office under the direction of Paul K. Knight.

Our firm made an effort during the 1930's to work out, with Turquand, Youngs & Co., the basis for a worldwide firm, but the thinking at the time was toward a separate firm to handle work outside the United States and Great Britain, or possibly an affiliation of a number of firms into a joint undertaking. The two were considering the formation of a worldwide firm when World War II commenced and the plans for an international practice were deferred. The war brought about a complete disruption of the continental practice, and when France fell, the Paris office of Turquand, Youngs & Co. was essentially abandoned. Their offices in the Far East were closed by the Japanese invasion, and their London practice was seriously disrupted by the Battle of Britain and by the heavy loss of personnel to the armed forces.

In Canada, Riddell, Stead, Graham & Hutchison played an important role in the early efforts of Arthur Andersen & Co. to serve the expanding operations of its clients. In 1932, the two firms commenced to represent each other in their respective countries, an arrangement that was to continue until the 1960's. The firm's affiliations with Fuller, King & Co. in Australia and Nils Olsson in Sweden also began in the 1930's.

END OF WORLD WAR II TO THE MID-1950's

This was an interim period which commenced with a continuation of the representation arrangements and ended with the conviction that we should establish our own overseas offices. It was notable as the period during which the firm tried out and discarded the joint undertaking approach to international operations.

Within a few months after hostilities ceased in Europe, the firm set about picking up the pieces of its prewar ideas. This responsibility was assigned to George Wagner, who saw, with prophetic vision, the growing need for our services in Europe following the end of World War II. Mr. Wagner remained in charge of our operations outside of the United States for about ten years and was also in charge of our New York office from 1950 to 1962.

Under the arrangement worked out in Europe by Mr. Wagner in 1945, experienced personnel of the firm were to transfer to Europe to supervise work performed by Turquand, Youngs for our United States clients. Turquand, Youngs assigned to one of its partners the primary responsibility for the Arthur Andersen & Co. work in England, reestablished its Paris office, made plans to send several of its people to the United States for training with our firm, and began again to represent us in South America and the Far East.

Many persons have transferred from their home countries, usually for limited periods, to further the development of our operations outside the United States. The first were Mark Littler, who went to London in December, 1945, to direct the work in England and on the Continent in cooperation with Turquand, Youngs & Co., and Joseph Sullivan, a commercial manager in the New York office, who transferred to Paris in the same month. The early days after the war were very difficult, but within a few months we were rendering service to our European clients.

Mr. Littler's report on the first six months' operations contained the following paragraphs describing our difficulties, progress and hopes:

" . . . *The first order of business was to supervise the carrying out of the 1945 audits on a basis consistent with our own standards. This was relatively less difficult in England than in Paris where the technical problems were much greater due to a five-year lapse in auditing and to general conditions arising out of the war. Records had been altered to confuse the Germans, innumerable laws were being passed from day to day to cope with postwar problems, national currencies had been seriously deranged, and inflation and black markets stalked the Continent. . . . The burden at Paris was further increased by the physical hardships arising from national shortages of food and fuel. The only heat in our own office was provided by two small wood stoves, and it was frequently necessary for our representatives to work in clients' offices without any heat at all in cold weather.*

"In spite of all the problems involved, it is believed that a creditable showing has been made. Delivery deadlines were met on all jobs for which delivery dates had been specified, and various technical problems overlooked in previous years were given more adequate attention.

*   *   *   *

"Only time will tell what Europe's future is to be, but at least we cannot hope for a peaceful and prosperous world unless we have a peaceful and prosperous Europe. Let us hope that some day it can be said that we, as a firm, through a professional practice anchored on integrity and high principle, played our part in helping a better Europe to rise from the rubble and travail that are hers today."

Kenneth M. Montgomery succeeded Mr. Littler as the firm's European partner in September, 1948. As of January 1, 1949, the joint arrangement was formalized by the formation of Arthur Andersen, Turquand, Youngs & Co. to handle the work of the two firms on the Continent, the United States work in England, Scotland, and Ireland, and the English assignments in the United States. This firm established offices in London, Paris, and New York. In Paris, all of the personnel were employed by the new firm, while in London the personnel were borrowed from the Turquand organization.

The composition of the Paris office during this time is of interest, both as to geographic coverage and personnel. During the period from 1948 to 1957, the Paris office was responsible for all work in most of Continental Europe, the north coast of Africa, and the Middle East. This vast territory with its many languages necessitated the employment of multilingual personnel. In 1953, the Paris office had a total complement of thirty-three—sixteen French, six English, five Swiss, four American, one Italian, and one Canadian. About half of the work of the office was outside of France.

In 1946, an arrangement for serving clients in Mexico was made with Roberto Casas Alatriste, a well-known educator and practitioner in México City. In essence, Arthur Andersen & Co. operated a department of that practice under the direct supervision of John H. Lumpkin.

During this period from the end of World War II to the mid-1950's, the firm continued its relations with Riddell, Stead, Graham & Hutchison (Canada), Fuller, King & Co. (Australia), and Nils Olsson (Sweden) and entered into arrangements with other firms throughout the world in order to serve American clients. These firms included Kontinentale Treuhandgesellschaft (Germany), Salas y Gutiérrez Gamoneda (Cuba), Hunter, Smith & Earle (Trinidad and Venezuela), and Saba & Co. (Lebanon).

MID-1950's TO THE PRESENT TIME

Through the years it had been difficult to administer our overseas work and maintain the firm's technical and service standards. Each move toward closer supervision of the work of our United States clients had been made to ease these difficulties. By the mid-1950's, developments justified full-scale offices in several areas, and the establishment of fully integrated Arthur Andersen & Co. offices was begun.

The joint arrangements in Mexico were discontinued in 1955 and our own office was established in Mexico City. In 1957, the arrangement with Turquand, Youngs in Europe was discontinued and our own offices were opened in Brussels, London, Milan, Oslo and Paris.

Our First London Office as seen from the proximity of the ruins of the ancient Roman wall

Our First Paris Office

Our growth in the United States had been almost entirely without acquisitions and mergers. However, in starting a practice in a new country, it appeared desirable to have a nucleus of personnel familiar with the language and business customs, and this sometimes necessitated the acquisition or merger of well-established, reputable local practices. This decision also was compatible with our philosophy that a practice should be built on the nationals of the country, and that non-nationals should be used only to the extent necessary to train the nationals in our policies, auditing procedures and accounting concept. At about this time the Turquand, Youngs practice in Brazil, Argentina and Uruguay was acquired, although offices were not established in Argentina and Uruguay until 1959. In 1958, we acquired the Venezuelan practice of Hunter, Smith & Earle and also commenced operations in Colombia.

São Paulo Office Location, 1957

From 1960 through 1963, the firm took the following steps in the further expansion of its overseas arrangements:

1. We entered into a representation agreement with Coopers & Lybrand under which the firm handled the Coopers & Lybrand work in South America and Coopers & Lybrand handled the firm's work in most of Africa. This constituted an exception to our established method of operation and the arrangement was discontinued in 1970.

2. Our efforts to develop a closer tie with Riddell, Stead, Graham & Hutchison proved unsuccessful and the decision was finally made to open Arthur Andersen & Co. offices in Canada. Under the new arrangement, an office was opened in Toronto in 1960 to handle our clients' work in that area and to coordinate for a period of years the firm's work handled by Riddell, Stead, Graham & Hutchison throughout the remainder of Canada.

3. The practice of Robinson & Paredes in Chile was acquired and offices established in that country and in Peru.

4. Offices were opened in Frankfurt/Main, The Hague, Zurich, Tokyo and Hamburg.

5. In 1961, the firm of Fuller, King & Co. in Australia, with offices in Melbourne, Sydney and Perth, became an integral part of our worldwide organization.

The merger with Fuller, King & Co. was the natural result of a long and close relationship between our two firms. In 1937, C. B. Harvey, a partner of Fuller, King & Co., made a trip to the United States. While he was in Chicago he made the acquaintance of Mr. Andersen and a representation agreement was worked out. The Fuller, King firm originated in 1894, nineteen years before the founding of Arthur Andersen & Co., but its growth occurred largely after World War II, with the growth of Australia's economy and population. The total personnel in 1946 was thirty-one, but by 1961 it had increased to approximately one hundred seventy. The oldest Melbourne client is Buckley & Nunn Ltd., a department store, which has been served since 1894.

For many years Frank Collinge, then a partner in the New York office, had been concerned with overseas work through his client responsibilities. After the war, he assisted in supervising firm personnel in Europe and Mexico and in establishing relations and maintaining liaison with firms throughout the world. With the development of our present concept of worldwide operations, he was transferred to Chicago in 1958 and was assigned the responsibility for establishing offices in the principal commercial areas outside of the United States. By 1962, when he asked to be relieved of his responsibilities, offices had been opened in many of the commercial centers of the world.

In 1963, twenty-six Arthur Andersen & Co. offices were in operation outside of the United States (shown by dates of establishment):

México City	1955	Montevideo	1959
Brussels	1957	Frankfurt	1960
London	1957	Lima	1960
Milan	1957	Santiago	1960
Oslo	1957	Toronto	1960
Paris	1957	Valparaiso	1960
Rio de Janeiro	1957	The Hague	1961
Santos	1957	Melbourne	1961
São Paulo	1957	Perth	1961
Bogotá	1958	Sydney	1961
Caracas	1958	Tokyo	1962
Maracaibo	1958	Zurich	1962
Buenos Aires	1959	Hamburg	1963

Mr. Collinge's responsibilities were largely taken over by Wayne E. O'Quinn who had worked closely with Mr. Collinge and who had been involved particularly in the development of our practice in South America. Walter Oliphant also took an increasingly active part in our international operations upon his election as managing partner in 1963.

The next ten years from 1964 to 1973 witnessed a further significant growth in our operations outside the United States with the opening of twenty-six additional offices and with substantial increases in the size of existing offices. Only two of these represented acquisitions of local practices—Vancouver in 1967 and Winnipeg in 1970, thus continuing our long-standing tradition of growing from within. In Vancouver, we acquired the practice of McIntosh, McVicar, Dinsley & Co. with a total personnel of seventy-two, and in Winnipeg, the practice of Nitikman, Linhart & Co. with thirty-seven people.

The twenty-six offices opened during the ten-year period from 1964 to 1973 (by dates of establishment) are as follows:

Madrid	1964	Recife	1967
Rome	1964	Vancouver	1967
Adelaide	1965	Athens	1968
Brisbane	1965	Dublin	1969
Cali	1965	Stockholm	1969
Johannesburg	1966	Barcelona	1970
Copenhagen	1966	Geneva	1970
Manchester	1966	Stuttgart	1970
Belo Horizonte	1967	Winnipeg	1970
Calgary	1967	Duesseldorf	1972
Glasgow	1967	Hong Kong	1972
Guayaquil	1967	Singapore	1972
Montreal	1967	Guadalajara	1973

As could be expected during a period of rapid political and economic change in certain parts of the world in the last ten years, there were bound to be some casualties. In Chile, for example, a decision was reached reluctantly to close our offices in that country—Valparaiso essentially in 1968 and Santiago in 1971. In 1969, the work of our office in Montevideo, Uruguay was taken over by our Buenos Aires office.

For a different reason, the Santos office was merged into the nearby São Paulo office in 1967. This office, which had been taken over from Turquand, Youngs as part of our acquisition of their practice in Brazil in 1957, served only São Paulo's port city and its further continuation as a separate operation could not be justified. Also, in 1970, the work in Maracaibo was absorbed by the Caracas office.

The spectacular growth in our international organization beginning in the mid-1950's had required a heavy investment by the partners, especially in normal start-up costs and in the recruiting and training of personnel. The principal emphasis necessarily had been on the development of people and the maintenance of the quality of our work. Now the time had come to put it all together as a coordinated and smooth-running whole.

Mr. Kapnick called on Robert I. Jones to assume that responsibility in 1970 as vice-chairman for international operations; under his leadership, our non-U.S. practice achieved a new measure of fulfillment and increasing recognition throughout the world.

By 1973, forty-seven non-U.S. offices were in operation with a total personnel of 3,484 in the following categories:

Partners and principals	184
Managers	515
Professional staff	2,050
Office support	735
Total	3,484

In addition, we developed arrangements for direct service to our clients in other important areas of the world where we do not have our own offices. Our joint undertakings with Saba & Co. (Lebanon) have continued to expand until today we have a joint firm, Arthur Andersen, Saba & Co., operating in three countries in the Middle East. This firm has three partners from Saba & Co. and three from Arthur Andersen & Co. and follows the same high standards of performance as other Arthur Andersen & Co. offices around the world.

In 1972, an Agreement for Professional Practice Collaboration was entered into with the SGV Group, which enables us to provide service to our clients having operations in Southeast Asia and Taiwan. The SGV Group was founded in Manila in 1946 by Mr. Washington SyCip and has been performing services for our clients since the 1950's. After starting in the Philippines, the SGV Group expanded to include member firms in Taiwan, Singapore, Indonesia, Malaysia, Thailand and Vietnam.

Although we opened our own office in Stockholm in 1969, our long-standing relationship with Nils Olsson still continues to supplement the services offered to our clients in Sweden.

Our most recent move in the international field has been the opening of our office in Moscow, USSR. Beginning in 1973, Mr. Kapnick, Mr. Jones and others held several meetings with government officials in both Russia and the USA and a Protocol was signed with the State Committee of the USSR Council of Ministers for Science and Technology, agreeing to cooperate and exchange technological knowledge in various areas. This was the first such agreement between the USSR and a professional accounting firm.

The first important exchange under this agreement was a five-day seminar conducted in Moscow by our representatives in October, 1973. This seminar was designed to explain to interested Soviet officials the scope and nature of the professional services our firm would be able to offer in the USSR and to provide a forum for our first discussion of the topics contemplated in the agreement.

Official accreditation and permission to establish our office in Moscow was received formally on April 29, 1974. Mr. George Kaiser, formerly of our Milwaukee office, will be the managing partner and the office will include a small staff of bilingual Soviet professional and office personnel supplemented by Arthur Andersen & Co. personnel from other offices as required.

This new office will enable us to assist our many clients around the world who are entering into trade and cooperation agreements with the Soviets and it will facilitate the carrying out of our long-term technical cooperation agreement with the USSR. It will begin an exciting new chapter since it means that our worldwide organization, which already encompassed many languages and cultures, will now include operations within the communist countries.

ГОСУДАРСТВЕННЫЙ КОМИТЕТ СОВЕТА МИНИСТРОВ СССР ПО НАУКЕ И ТЕХНИКЕ		STATE COMMITTEE OF USSR COUNCIL OF MINISTERS FOR SCIENCE AND TECHNOLOGY

11, GORKY STREET, MOSCOW. TEL. 29-22-36

Р А З Р Е Ш Е Н И Е

Государственный комитет Совета Министров СССР по науке и технике разрешает американской фирме "Артур Андерсен" открыть в Москве представительство под наименованием "Представительство фирмы "Артур Андерсен" в Москве" с целью надлежащего выполнения обязательств фирмы по соглашениям о научно-техническом и экономическом сотрудничестве, подписанным с Госкомитетом и другими советскими организациями.

Представительство ежеквартально, к 10 числу месяца, следующего за истекшим кварталом, представляет в Протокольный отдел Государственного комитета Совета Министров СССР по науке и технике отчет, предусмотренный инструкцией "О порядке выдачи разрешений на открытие представительств иностранных фирм в СССР и регулировании их деятельности".

Число сотрудников Представительства из числа американских граждан - служащих фирмы, включая главу Представительства, не должно превышать двух человек.

Разрешение действительно на срок до 29 апреля 1975 года.

Начальник Протокольного
отдела

/Г.Котов/

N 121

"__" апреля 1974 г.

МПФГ. 1972. Зак. 18271.

Accreditation to open an office in Moscow, USSR

CHAPTER EIGHT

The Three Divisions of Our Practice

EARLY IDENTIFICATION OF OUR THREE AREAS OF PRACTICE

The identification of the three major areas of our professional practice, i.e., auditing, taxes and administrative services, had an early beginning, having been described separately in Mr. Andersen's announcement of the opening of his practice on December 1, 1913. In brief, this announcement (see page 3) referred to the services to be offered in the areas of:

Periodical audits, the certification of financial statements and special investigations

The design and installation of new systems

The preparation of reports under the Federal income tax law

AUDITING—THE FOCAL PART OF OUR PRACTICE

Auditing has always constituted the focal part of our practice and much of the material in this volume is naturally related to the development of the audit division which, traditionally, accounts for about two thirds of our total fees. In the earlier years, Mr. Andersen, himself, was actively involved in the audit function. As the practice grew, the responsibilities for control of quality and for the technical aspects of our audit work were delegated to others. Such men as Grant Chandler, Charles W. Jones, Eric Kohler and Newton V. Wagner were involved at one time or another. Mr. Jones emerged as the senior technician with his appointment as chairman of the Committee on Accounting Principles and Auditing Procedures (see Chapter Ten).

In 1941, Hugh E. Nichols was selected by Mr. Andersen to head our firmwide commercial audit practice—a position that he filled until his retirement in 1967. For many years, Mr. Nichols regularly visited all of the firm's offices and held personal interviews with practically every partner and manager. He became a familiar figure throughout the organization and his sage advice was sought by many.

In 1965, John W. March, who was the Managing Partner of the Boston office was called to Chicago to work with Mr. Nichols, whom he succeeded in 1967. The continuing growth of our practice required a further strengthening of the administration of our audit function and this was accomplished through the appointment of practice directors as described more fully in Chapter Ten.

Our tax and administrative services divisions also have played important roles in the firm and there are a number of matters of historical interest in the development of these two divisions.

TAXES

Income taxes did not have a significant impact on the practice until World War I when income tax rates were increased substantially and a war-time excess profits tax was inaugurated. As already indicated, Mr. Andersen's special course in income taxes at Northwestern University in

1917-18 attracted a large enrollment including prominent business executives, bankers and lawyers, and it was only natural that many of these people and their associates would turn to Mr. Andersen and his organization for assistance.

At that time, the tax return audit function of the then Bureau of Internal Revenue was all administered through its National office in Washington, D. C. The work of internal revenue agents was supervised and reviewed there, appeal hearings on issues raised by field agents were held there, and technical issues raised by taxpayers and field agents were decided there. It soon became obvious that direct and continuing access to the National office of the Bureau would greatly facilitate and improve service to clients on work relating to revenue agents' examinations and in obtaining rulings on tax questions important to our clients.

To meet this need, a small office was opened in Washington on January 1, 1921. This was the third office to be opened by the firm and it was to continue primarily as a tax service oriented office for many years.

Edwin D. Evans, who joined the organization in 1923, later succeeded Walter Andersen as the partner in charge of taxes and remained in this position until his resignation in 1943. Michael J. Sporrer was named as his successor with instructions from Arthur Andersen to build a strong and self-contained tax group in each operating office. Mr. Sporrer had come to the organization only eight years earlier from a private practice in law and tax accounting and from 1937 to 1938 he had been in charge of the Washington office. Although quiet and unassuming, he had great personal warmth, and in addition to his extensive knowledge of income taxes, he brought to the position tremendous dedication and drive. The results were soon reflected in an acceleration of the growth of our income tax organization and total tax fees. Our tax practice has continued to grow in tandem with our expanding auditing practice. Mr. Sporrer served as head of the tax division until 1958, when he was followed, in turn, by Clarence F. McCarthy, John R. Mendenhall and Donald M. Gamet.

Over the years, the general nature of our tax practice has changed substantially. Our work relating to the filing of required reports with the taxing authorities has become much less dominant and much of it has shifted from filling out official tax forms to providing input needed for computer preparation of returns, to assisting clients in automating their own compliance procedures and to reviewing the technical adequacy and completeness of returns prepared by clients. Assistance to clients related to revenue agents' reports and ruling requests has grown apace with the increasing size and complexity of business. With this, too, has come a rapidly increasing need by clients for competent tax help in planning major transactions; for assistance in utilizing the provisions of tax statutes to help solve major business problems; and for an independent outside source of information as to differences between the company's tax accounting and financial accounting methods, the adequacy and defensibility of its tax procedures and the amount and timing of its potential tax exposures.

Our tax practice in many other countries has developed more slowly due to less sophisticated income tax laws, local customs and other factors but there are well established tax divisions in most offices and the geographic scope of our tax practice is increasing annually as more governments move to refine their tax structures and collection procedures.

ADMINISTRATIVE SERVICES

The development of our administrative services practice followed a somewhat different pattern. As set forth in Chapter Two, early in its history the firm developed an excellent reputation for financial investigations which were used particularly by investment bankers in connection with public offerings. These investigations utilized both accounting and engineering skills and, as a result, certain of the individuals involved were predominantly engineering oriented. With the crash of 1929, financing engagements dwindled, and this type of work was essentially discontinued in 1930.

For a period of time thereafter, those men in the organization with engineering skills continued to perform more routine systems engagements, but gradually the systems specialists dropped out and by the late 1930s and early 1940s, the auditing organization was responsible for carrying out the systems work being generated.

It was World War II that indirectly prompted a major change in the direction of our systems work. The importance of data processing to the logistics of the war brought about two very important developments with respect to accounting for business enterprises. The first was a new and more favorable attitude on the part of businessmen toward the mechanization of accounting and related clerical work, and the second was an increased respect for the extent to which data gathering and accounting analysis could be used to operate a business enterprise more intelligently and effectively.

During the war, military and governmental units were always operating against deadlines. In order to gain time, they were forced to mechanize a substantial part of their data-gathering and accounting activities. This enabled them to produce results in a relatively shorter time than would otherwise have been possible and to conserve clerical labor, which was in very short supply. Many former businessmen who were active in the government service during the war were obtaining extensive and enlightening experience in mechanizing every possible type of accounting and clerical routine. Naturally, upon returning to civilian life, these men brought with them a new respect for mechanized accounting, and subsequently went about in their own companies in search of opportunities for reducing their clerical effort. This process was further accelerated by the rapid postwar inflation which was especially evident in clerical salary levels.

Many of these same businessmen, while in wartime service, also developed a materially changed attitude toward the importance of a discriminating analysis of past operations as a guide to effective future action. Because of the magnitude of the governmental wartime operations which they were supervising, these men were forced to rely on accounting and statistical analyses and reports when making decisions. In many cases, this was a rather dramatic change from the "seat of the pants" type of operation with which they had previously been familiar in business life. Thus, the businessman returning to civilian life found himself very much dissatisfied with the old prewar methods he had employed and began to demand accounting and statistical reports that could help him run his business more efficiently. This need was further accentuated by the substantial post-war growth in the size of many business entities.

Naturally, these changed attitudes of the businessman were bound to bring about a significant change in what he expected from his accountants. He expected competent assistance in the mechanization of accounting and clerical routines, and he expected that his accountants would be able to guide and help him in making his accounting and reporting system more useful as a management tool.

The management of our firm recognized the inevitability of this development before the conclusion of the war and set about laying plans for developing competence in these new areas. It was concluded that a new operating division should be organized under the name of "administrative accounting" which was changed two years later to "administrative services."

To head this new division, the firm called on James A. Campbell, who was brought to Chicago from New York in 1942. Mr. Campbell had had a wide experience in the firm, having worked in auditing and income taxes as well as in systems work; but especially it was recognized that he had the talents needed to get the new division into operation.

The name of the new division had been chosen carefully to distinguish the character of its work from the so-called "management services" type of work being performed by other organizations. Because of responsibilities as independent public accountants, it was concluded that we could not become involved in work where our personnel were, in effect, making management decisions for a client. Our work was to be involved in all those areas relating to the development and gathering of information used as tools by management in operating their businesses and in making business decisions, but we, ourselves, could not be making those decisions.

Also, in establishing and building our administrative services division, the firm did not follow the practice of some other firms of building to a great extent with specialists obtained from outside the organization. Our approach was to employ a relatively few top-notch, highly trained men and to concentrate on building from within, through the intensive training of competent personnel of our own who were already well trained in accounting and auditing and who had a good general knowledge of business methods. This approach required a substantial investment in training, but the results obtained justified the cost. Within a period of four or five years, the administrative services division had developed a high degree of competence.

Furthermore, by building from within, the firm avoided the inherent tendency for such a department to operate independently and to become isolated from its audit and tax divisions. From the inception of the development of special work, the firm has approached it from the standpoint that all such work was to have the benefit of the combined talents of the organization. This involved bringing to bear all of our accounting, audit and tax competence on each engagement of the administrative services division. We wanted to integrate administrative services with our over-all services to clients and to avoid the pitfall, common to this type of professional work, of developing a firm within a firm.

This integration was later to become more formalized (in 1972) with the adoption of a policy requiring the organization of so-called "client service teams" for all major audit clients. Traditionally, these client service teams are comprised of representatives of our three divisions (audit, tax and administrative services) who, among other things, coordinate all phases of our work for each respective client.

Two key additions were made to the personnel of this department in 1946 when John A. Higgins returned from wartime service with the U.S. Navy and Joseph S. Glickauf was employed upon his release from the Navy. Mr. Higgins was later to succeed Mr. Campbell as head of the division when, in 1951, Mr. Campbell was transferred to Los Angeles to become the partner in charge of that office. When Mr. Higgins was named director of administration for the firm in 1957 (see page 71), Mr. Glickauf succeeded Mr. Higgins as head of the division and remained in that capacity until 1969 when he was succeeded by William C. Ingersoll who, in turn, was followed by William J. Mueller in 1971.

With the end of the war, we began to become involved with the impact of punched cards on our clients' accounting and reporting systems as distinct from their prewar use principally as a means for performing relatively simple statistical and analytical work. Our work grew rapidly as new concepts were developed for better control of costs and assets through greater mechanization utilizing punched cards, and by the 1950's we had begun to build our administrative services competence in offices outside of Chicago.

In the late forties, the development of electronic computers for businesses began to take shape. Mr. Glickauf was assigned to explore this new and reportedly revolutionary development and, in the process, visited universities and laboratories. Mr. Glickauf's notes contain the following paragraph concerning his inspection of an early prototype at the University of Pennsylvania:

"The demonstration we were given was impressive, if brief. But it took no genius to see that we had before us a device that

would outrun, outpower and outmode every device that preceded it. I left Philadelphia with a mission. It was to convince everyone I encountered, not only within the firm but also without, that this day I had indeed seen a vision of what would soon become a revolutionary reality."

Mr. Glickauf determined then and there to build his own model which would illustrate the operation and the speed of this new device and before long this model became familiar around the whole firm and among our clients.

Mr. Glickauf and the computer model he built and used
for demonstration purposes

During this period, meetings were arranged with representatives of a number of major computer manufacturers who opined that we were wasting our time as they had already satisfied themselves that our objectives of a broad application of computers for business use were not practical. Nevertheless, in 1952 we were engaged by General Electric Company to assist them in the possible adaptation of a computer to their own accounting system in a new and modern plant already constructed at Appliance Park in Kentucky. The company wanted to have an advanced accounting system to match its advanced manufacturing techniques. Out of this engagement there emerged the first major computer applications for the processing and recording of business transactions. This was a milestone event in the development of computers for business use as well as in the development of our administrative services practice, and it marked the beginning of a dramatic firm-wide growth in our practice. Virtually all phases of accounting and data processing came within the computer's scope and thus old friends developed in the punched card accounting era (such as responsibility accounting, production and inventory control, management information systems and accounting controls) became even more in demand as more sophisticated equipment became available.

In 1956, Mr. Glickhauf was given the responsibility for starting our administrative services practice outside the United States. As a first step, Arthur Welby was sent to the Milan office to employ and train administrative services personnel locally, and for a period of time our systems work in Europe was performed out of that office. By 1960, Mr. Welby was able to return to the United States, having developed a group to carry on without his direction. In 1957, Frank Dwiggins was transferred from the Chicago office to the London office to direct our administrative services practice in the United Kingdom. Today, the London office has the third largest administrative services group in the firm. The Paris office is not far behind, with its early development having been directed by Guy Barbier followed by Pierre Réveillion.

In 1973, the administrative services division had grown to a total of almost 1,500 people with annual fees of approximately $42 million. We believe that our administrative services division, which traditionally accounts for about 15% of the firm's total annual fees, is the largest organization of its kind in the world today.

CHAPTER NINE

The Evolution of Our Administrative Structure

From the founding of the firm on December 1, 1913, until his death in 1947, Arthur Andersen had remained the dominant figure in the organization. As already indicated, he had a peculiar genius for surrounding himself with outstanding people and placing them in positions of responsibility. At the same time, he administered the firm with a strong hand; his basic philosophy of a strong centralized management was to continue after his death. The transition in leadership from Mr. Andersen to Leonard Spacek as managing partner, and Paul K. Knight and Charles W. Jones as chairman and vice-chairman of the partnership, has already been related in Chapter Five.

THE ADVISORY GROUP

In addition to the positions of managing partner and chairman and vice-chairman of the partnership, there was established an advisory group (later changed to advisory committee) elected by the partners and consisting of six partners, including the chairman and vice-chairman. The six members were divided into three classes of two each, with their three-year terms expiring in successive years in order to provide continuity. The initial members of the advisory group were F. Merrill Beatty, Renick H. Buckles, Charles W. Jones, Paul K. Knight, Hugh E. Nichols and George Wagner.

Initially, the advisory group was established to provide the new managing partner with a formal body of the firm's more experienced partners whose counsel he could seek on any matter. As its name implied, the group's function was only advisory. Mr. Spacek had made it clear at the outset that he would serve as managing partner only if he could have complete and final responsibility for the day-to-day management decisions.

In a few years, the confidence in Mr. Spacek's leadership had reached the point where the partners were agreeable to a change in the general character of the advisory group and the process was started of bringing into it younger partners who showed particular promise for the future. These younger men were thus able to share a period of valuable training by being intimately exposed to the firm's operations.

AN ORGANIZATION PLAN TAKES FORM

A more formal organization plan soon evolved. The delegation of authority by the partners to the elected managing partner was very definite and complete. The managing partner, in turn, appointed a line and staff management organization to assist him in running the firm. The line management organization consisted of the managing partner, the directors of United States and overseas operations and the partners in charge of offices. All line authority rested with the managing partner who, in turn, delegated it to the partners occupying the designated positions. The intent was not to add extra layers of supervision; rather, it was to provide a vehicle through which the managing partner could delegate his authority.

In addition to the line organization, the managing partner obtained assistance through the staff or functional management group, which consisted of the director of industry competence, the partners in charge of quality control on a firm-wide basis for audit, taxes and administrative services, the directors of personnel and training and the Committee on Accounting Principles and Auditing Procedures (see page 81). Those partners with functional responsibility operated as right arms of the managing partner in their particular fields but did not exercise line authority from the standpoint of having operating areas reporting directly to them, as did the directors of operations.

The responsibility of administering our rapidly expanding organization, along with a heavy involvement in the professional side of the practice, began to place inordinate demands on Mr. Spacek's time. To meet this situation, the office of director of administration was created in 1957 with the provision that its incumbent, to be elected by the partners, would report directly to the managing partner and would have a major responsibility for the day-to-day administration of the firm.

On Mr. Spacek's recommendation, John A. Higgins was elected as the first director of administration. This was a fortuitous choice. Mr. Higgins had already distinguished himself as the head of the firm's administrative services practice. His aggressive, courageous leadership and his insistence upon perfection were combined with human understanding and good humor which endeared him to all who worked with him. He served in this capacity until his untimely death in 1965. Few men have had a greater impact on the firm.

THE BOARD OF DIRECTORS

With one major exception, the firm operated essentially under this organization plan until 1970 when Harvey Kapnick was elected as managing partner to succeed Walter Oliphant. The one major change was the introduction of a board of directors in 1968, to take the place of the advisory group, with the concurrent redefinition of certain of the responsibilities of the managing partner. By this time, the firm had grown to a point where the partners believed that a broader group should be brought into the policy-making process. The board was composed of twelve partners, elected by the partnership, and was given the responsibility for approving recommendations on policy made by the managing partner, screening candidates for partnership, selecting the nominees for succeeding managing partners and recommending changes in agreements among partners. Donald J. Erickson was elected as chairman and continued to serve in that capacity until March 31, 1974.

A NEW MANAGING PARTNER (1963)

Following an established tradition in the firm that its administration should be kept in young hands, Mr. Spacek stepped aside as managing partner on December 1, 1963, at the age of 56, in order to concentrate his work on the professional side of our practice and on his continuing efforts to bring the profession in the United States forward in its formulation and adoption of sound accounting principles. He was immediately elected to a newly created position of chairman of the partners—a post he continued to fill until 1970 when he became a senior partner.

Walter Oliphant, at the age of 46, was elected as managing partner to succeed Mr. Spacek. He, too, had risen through the ranks, having started in the Chicago office as a staff accountant in 1939. After serving as partner in charge of the Boston office from 1953 to 1959, he had returned to Chicago in the latter year to become director of United States and Canadian operations. In this capacity, he had worked very closely with Mr. Spacek and thus had gained an intimate knowledge of the firm's operations and practices. After a careful screening of potential candidates by an ad hoc committee of partners, his was the only name submitted by the committee to the annual meeting of the partners in 1963.

HARVEY KAPNICK SUCCEEDS WALTER OLIPHANT AS MANAGING PARTNER

In 1969, after six years as managing partner, Mr. Oliphant concluded that the responsibilities entailed in managing a worldwide professional organization of this size were so heavy that no one should be asked to carry such a burden for a period of more than six years. To give further substance to his views on this, Mr. Oliphant asked to be replaced as managing partner in 1970 and at his urging, the partnership agreement was amended in 1969 to provide that the term of office of a managing partner would be for a period of approximately six years (later revised to permit extensions for successive terms of up to three years each).

At their annual meeting in May, 1970, the partners elected Harvey Kapnick, at the age of 44, to be the firm's fourth managing partner. Mr. Oliphant was elected a senior partner.

Mr. Kapnick had experienced a rapid rise in the firm. Upon completion of his education after World War II, he had started in the Chicago office as a staff accountant. Only eight years later he had been admitted to the partnership and shortly thereafter was placed in charge of the merchandising industry division of the Chicago office. When elected as the firm's chief executive in 1970, he had been the managing partner of the Cleveland office for eight years and a member of the board of directors from the date of its inauguration in 1968. As a matter of fact, he had played a major role in the creation of the board as a policy body.

A NEW ORGANIZATION CONCEPT

Mr. Kapnick immediately embarked on a program to restructure our administrative organization. It still incorporated the basic line and staff philosophy but introduced numerous major revisions.

The title of the firm's chief executive was changed from managing partner to chairman and chief executive and the concept of the chairman's office was introduced to bring together into one group the following:

Chairman and chief executive

Chairman of the Committee on Accounting Principles and Auditing Procedures

Vice chairmen responsible for specified operational and functional areas of our practice—

Operational—
Administration
Chicago office
New York office
International

Functional—
Accounting and auditing practice
Tax practice
Administrative services practice

The key unit in the firm continued to be the individual office, and the title of the partner in charge of each office was changed to managing partner. As before, the managing partner of each operating office is responsible for implementing our objectives of client service, growth, profitability, development of our personnel and appropriate supervision over each client engagement.

A number of the firm's more experienced partners were selected to be responsible for the operation and administration of respective groups of designated offices, and these partners were given the title of country managing partner. Outside the United States, these office groups are largely geographical; in the United States, groups are determined by a number of factors in addition to geography. These country managing partners report directly to the chairman's office.

To be certain that our growing organization had the experience and competence to handle quickly the day-to-day professional practice questions that arise throughout the world, each functional vice chairman is assisted by practice directors who are located throughout the world to provide a fast response and a consistent approach to the understanding and handling of our clients' problems. The work of these practice directors is discussed more fully in the next chapter, which relates to our professional practice.

The concept of an advisory partner on each of our larger engagements was introduced. Advisory partners are assigned to assist engagement partners and to provide further flexibility and experience in dealing with the complex operations of these companies. This double team approach provides our clients with continuity, experienced judgment and rotation to assure independence and new ideas.

A new category of partner was established—the senior partner. This designation was to be reserved for individual partners who had achieved distinction throughout the firm and who had given up specific leadership positions as part of the plan to bring younger partners into those positions. Appointments to this category are made by the chairman and chief executive with the approval of the Board of Directors. By 1973, eight partners had been thus recognized—Albert J. Bows, Jr., James A. Campbell, Lloyd I. Coveney, John L. Hennessy, Mark Littler, Edward E. Maltby, Walter Oliphant and Leonard Spacek.

In 1973, an advisory council comprised of thirty younger partners selected from our worldwide organization, was established as a vehicle to give the younger partnership group an opportunity to work together, to study various issues affecting the future of the firm and to increase the communication among the younger men relating to the fundamental and philosophical issues facing the firm in the ensuing five to ten years. Those eligible for selection to the council must have been partners for at least two years and not more than eight years. The council has its own chairman (Duane Kullberg) and vice chairmen (James Hanson and Lawrence Weinbach) and a committee structure. It holds regular meetings, but it has no direct responsibility for firm policies.

All of the various parts work closely together as a coordinated whole. This is exemplified by the new organization chart designed by Mr. Kapnick which takes the form of a wheel whose center is the Chairman's Office— directing and coordinating all activities and functions and maintaining open lines of communication to all members of our entire worldwide organization.

Three years of operation under this new organization plan have already proved its soundness. It continues our long-established policy of strong centralized management and further strengthens our one-firm concept. Moreover, it is flexible and offers a whole new base for the continued expansion of our organization that is bound to come. It has proved to be another milestone in our first sixty years.

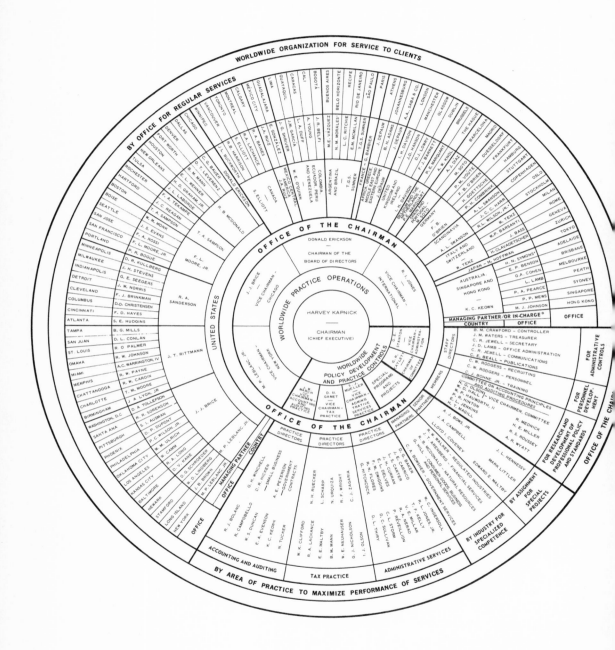

Firm Organization Chart—1973

OUR COMPUTER—A NEW MANAGEMENT TOOL

The effectiveness of this enlarged centralized administration has been enhanced by the utilization of an important management tool—the computerization of most of our financial and operating information. As related elsewhere, the firm had pioneered in developing the application of computers to business systems and it seemed appropriate to adapt these new techniques to our own management needs. Although business computers became commonplace in the next decade, the concept was still in its earlier stages at this point in time.

In 1964, a task force under John Higgins had been asked to make a thorough study as to the feasibility of a computer for the firm and this group recommended that the firm proceed with the project. A team of computer specialists from the administrative services division under the supervision of John Spellman was assigned to the work and on October 1, 1967, the entire accounting function (including payrolls, work in progress, accounts receivable and the complete general ledger for all offices in the United States, Canada and Puerto Rico) was cut over to the new computer system. The central processing unit is housed in Chicago and pertinent management reports are distributed to the various offices for use on a responsibility basis. For all offices outside the United States, a second computer center was established in Milan, Italy, and the last international office was added to that computer in 1973.

A SPECIAL TRIBUTE TO TWO MEMBERS OF OUR ADMINISTRATIVE STAFF

Any review of the evolution of our administrative organization would be incomplete without special mention of the contribution made by two members of our staff—Miss Beatrice Olsen and Mrs. Byford Heskett (Miss Mildred Baker).

Miss Olsen, who joined us in 1926, was Arthur Andersen's secretary until his death in 1947. Subsequently, she became the assistant secretary and assistant treasurer of the firm, a post she held until her retirement in 1967. Her thorough, competent handling of the firm's multitudinous documents and records kept the wheels of the organization running smoothly. She was possessed of exceptional qualities and was a tremendously valuable member of our organization.

Mrs. Heskett, who began her career with the firm in 1935, was one of Mr. Andersen's secretaries for several years. She became the secretary to Leonard Spacek in 1947, the year of his selection as managing partner of the firm, and she served in that capacity until Mr. Spacek's retirement in 1973. Mrs. Heskett was familiar with every facet of the firm's operations and with her initiative and good judgment she was able personally to dispose of many of the day-to-day problems coming to the managing partner's office. She earned a most enviable reputation by the tact, efficiency and dispatch with which she discharged the myriad duties of her position. She retired from active duty at the end of 1973.

Both Miss Olsen and Mrs. Heskett were elected honorary partners at the time of their retirement.

OUR OFFICE SUPPORT ORGANIZATION

These are but two examples of the tireless and dedicated efforts of our total office support group which forms another major segment of our administrative structure. A professional organization such as ours involves a tremendous amount of behind-the-scenes work in our continuing communication with clients and within our own organization, in printing and issuing our reports to clients, in maintaining the multitudinous records required in compliance with legal requirements and good business practice and in countless other areas of activity. The effective work of typists, secretaries, printers, receptionists and other specialists around the world in support of our professional activities has made a major contribution to the high level of client service that has come to be associated with the name of Arthur Andersen & Co.

CHAPTER TEN

Foundations of Professional Competence

From its beginning in 1913, the firm has enjoyed a reputation for integrity and forthrightness. Mr. Andersen, himself, personified these qualities, and his admonition to "think straight—talk straight" became a motto for the entire organization.

These qualities constituted a solid foundation on which to build the firm's reputation for sound auditing, but as the firm grew, much more had to be built into the superstructure to develop and expand our competence, to control the quality of our work and to unify our expanding worldwide practice into a cohesive whole. Some of the important steps taken to accomplish these objectives were:

- The development of the "one-firm" concept and, with this concept, the philosophy that the firm must speak with one voice;

- The organization of a separate committee to carry out research in the areas of accounting principles and auditing procedures;

- The encouragement of a business approach to auditing problems;

- The institution of new and improved methods of communication within the organization;

- The centralization of control over and the standardization of recruiting and training throughout the world;

- The improvement of our knowledge and competence along industry lines; and

- The selection of practice directors to assure a high level of professional performance in all areas of our practice.

THE "ONE-FIRM" CONCEPT AND SPEAKING WITH ONE VOICE

Fundamentally, a professional partnership is an association of individual entrepreneurs, each with his own clients, over which he hovers like a mother hen. The secret of building a firm rather than an association of individual practices lies in establishing and maintaining a "one-firm" concept to such a degree that it will override and take precedence over the basic tendency that is always present to operate independently. When a professional firm is small, it is not too difficult to weld a group into a solid organization which, although its members think independently, nevertheless speaks with one voice on matters involving important professional opinions. However, as a professional organization grows in size, nationally and internationally, the problem of "oneness" becomes increasingly difficult.

We believe we have maintained this "one-firm" concept, even in the face of the rapid growth over the past twenty-six years, and that its effect has become apparent in every major area of our operations. It has already been referred to in Chapter Seven concerning our development into a worldwide organization and in Chapter Nine on the evolution of our administrative structure. A further manifestation is to be found in our policy of speaking with one voice in our professional practice.

The firm adopted early in its history the policy that all partners would follow a common approach in dealing with any particular accounting problem and in their utterances outside the firm. As far as the public is concerned, it was essential to have one official viewpoint—to speak with one voice—on important matters involving accounting principles. This did not mean any lessening of freedom of discussion of controversial questions within the organization when an accounting policy or principle was being established. On the contrary, individual views were encouraged and differences in opinion were often heatedly argued, but once a majority position had been agreed upon, every partner was expected to uphold that position. This practice is so obviously sound that it has continued in full effect to the present time.

THE COMMITTEE ON ACCOUNTING PRINCIPLES AND AUDITING PROCEDURES

In order for the policy of speaking with one voice to be fully effective, it was essential that there be a framework within which the partners could discuss the pros and cons of a position before arriving at a decision binding on all of them. Such a framework is provided by the Committee on Accounting Principles and Auditing Procedures, whose history goes back almost to the beginning of the firm.

During the early years of the firm's existence, the group of partners and managers was small, and problems of an accounting or auditing nature were decided in informal discussions. As this group became larger and new offices were established across the country, periodic meetings of partners and managers became the vehicle for discussion of problems and dissemination of information. As the problems with respect to accounting and auditing became more numerous and more complex, they were assigned to committees for study.

A Committee on Technique, consisting of five members, was established in 1929 "to encourage and develop uniformity in audit procedures and reports." This committee issued bulletins to inform the organization of its conclusions in connection with the various problems studied. When a Managers' Manual was developed in 1933 for the purpose of gathering in one binder the bulletins and other memoranda previously issued to set forth the approved practices of the firm, the manual contained fifty bulletins that had been issued by the Committee on Technique. These bulletins were issued by the committee over the signatures of Newton V. Wagner, Grant Chandler or Eric L. Kohler, with the approval of Arthur Andersen or Charles W. Jones.

In 1937, the activities of the Committee on Technique were delegated to the partners in charge of our commercial and utility practice. However, the expansion of the firm's practice from 1937 to 1945 indicated the need for a more formal organization to consider accounting and auditing problems and to establish the policies of the firm in those areas, and in January, 1945, Arthur Andersen announced the re-establishment of the Committee on Technique. He described its enlarged purpose as follows:

> "*Broadly speaking, the functions of the committee are to promote the education and training of our men; to promote, direct and correlate sound thinking and research on accounting and auditing questions and statement presentation; and to mold the expressed results of the best thinking of the organization into clear statements of the firm's policies.*"

When this Committee was re-established, Mr. Andersen was chairman and Charles W. Jones was vice chairman. Shortly thereafter, Mr. Jones became chairman and served in that capacity until about 1957. In 1954, the name of the committee was changed to Committee on Accounting Principles and Auditing Procedures, in order to more accurately describe its purpose and to put less emphasis on the narrower concept of technique. Others who have served as chairman of the Committee since Mr. Jones are Richard C. Brandt, Russell H. Morrison and George R. Catlett, the present chairman, who was elected to that position in 1962.

The Committee is elected by and reports to the partners as well as to the chairman and chief executive on all matters. The number of persons on the committee is open and it grows with the volume of the work involved. At present, the Committee is comprised of eleven partners who devote full time to it. Other partners and managers work with the committee from time to time in carrying out its responsibilities.

One of the principal functions of the Committee is to consider all facets of an accounting principle or an auditing problem (including obtaining the opinions of partners best informed on the subject) and ultimately to issue a policy statement binding on all members of the organization.

The present series of Firm Accounting Releases was started in 1940 with the first one being on the subject of "Notices of Irregularities to Boards of Directors." This release is still in effect (with only minor revisions), and is just as applicable today as it was in 1940. Many other releases have been issued since that time. All releases are under continuous review and are revised or withdrawn as conditions or policies change.

One of the earlier releases on the form and content of auditors' reports was subsequently expanded into a separate book, *Auditors' Reports*. This book, which is updated periodically to keep pace with developments in the profession, now comprises almost 400 pages and is used extensively in our daily practice throughout the world. Another book to be released shortly, *Ethical Standards*, brings together in one place our policies relating to professional ethics, independence, scope of practice and conflicts of interest.

Policy statements are issued for each of the countries in which the firm has offices to cover special or unique problems in those countries.

The firm's basic policies on auditing procedures are stated in *Audit Objectives and Procedures*. This book, initially issued in 1943, serves as a general guide for many of the audit problems that arise on an audit engagement, but it is not intended as a manual of rules to be followed without the use of judgment. The latest edition of this book (now 546 pages) was issued in 1961. It is currently in the process of being revised again with the assistance of a number of partners and managers.

The Committee is constantly studying the auditing procedures being followed throughout the firm. This is done in part through the review of case reports submitted for inclusion in the Subject File (see page 86) and the program for review of audit engagements discussed below.

There is, of course, a continuing need to adapt our auditing procedures to changing conditions. The growth of the use of computers in business, described in Chapter Eight, also offered the auditor an opportunity to introduce a degree of automation into his procedures. In the late 1960's, under the general supervision of the Committee, the firm developed a generalized computer audit package which we call AUDEX, an acronym for AUDit EXtract system. The program's name describes its basic function: to extract data from a variety of client computer files and to process that data into formats best suited to the needs of each audit.

Although it is a highly sophisticated system, AUDEX is relatively easy to use and with a minimum of training, audit personnel very quickly become confident and competent in its use. AUDEX enables us to maximize the use of the computer in our audits.

An annual interoffice audit review program is conducted under the supervision of the Committee. Under this program, working papers and other aspects of audits at each office around the world are periodically reviewed on a selective-test basis by a partner or manager from another office. These reviews are an essential part of our quality control program designed to make certain that the standards prescribed for our audit work are consistently maintained.

The firm's practice as it relates to the Securities and Exchange Commission also represents an important phase of the Committee's activities. The Committee is generally responsible for establishing the firm's policies with respect to SEC practice just as it is responsible for establishing the firm's policies on other accounting matters. Further, members of the Committee confer with partners and managers throughout the firm on accounting and reporting matters currently under consideration by the SEC.

This Committee is a key instrument in maintaining our one-firm concept through its establishment of accounting policies and its program for quality control on a worldwide basis. In addition, the Committee is extensively engaged in research activities which are described more fully in Chapter Twelve, which deals with the firm's leadership role in the profession as a whole.

BUSINESS APPROACH TO AUDITING

From the beginning, Arthur Andersen placed great emphasis on the importance of a business approach to our auditing work—on getting and reporting the facts behind the figures. He talked about it, wrote about it and made speeches about it. Years later, Paul K. Knight (then a senior partner) was to write that, "As the older men in the organization well know, the basic idea of looking behind the figures and applying business sense to their translation into terms of the contributing factors has been the solid foundation on which Mr. Andersen has built the firm. . . ."

Mr. Andersen had a strong aversion to an audit performed without imagination and consisting almost entirely of routine audit checks. He never forgot that we were a service organization, and he rightly felt that our fees were justified by our constant alertness to discover deficiencies in the company's accounting procedures and practical methods of correcting these deficiencies.

Eventually, on January 5, 1939, he issued a bulletin initiating a policy of submitting informal memorandums of recommendations to clients. It read as follows:

> *"It will be a firm policy from this time forward, whenever an audit is made, to require the preparation of a memorandum of suggestions for improvements in the accounting methods and procedures, and with respect to any other accounting matters regarding which we can give constructive suggestions."*

These memorandums began to be called "Blueback Memorandums," since it became firm practice to attach them to a plain blue sheet of paper as a backing. The reaction of our clients has been uniformly favorable to this additional service. Frequently, they were of special interest to the chief executive. Usually the audit merely confirmed what he already knew, but the bluebacks were a "plus" factor, indicating that his public accountants were able to make practical suggestions regarding accounting and business matters. The requirement still exists that a blueback memorandum be prepared on each audit engagement or, if not prepared, that a memorandum be written to explain its absence.

COMMUNICATION WITHIN THE FIRM

The problem of maintaining effective communication within any organization, whether it be a corporation, partnership or individual proprietorship, is one that becomes increasingly complex and difficult as the organization grows in size. It is, however, particularly difficult in a partnership form of organization because of two aspects of the problem that ordinarily are not present in other forms of business organization.

The first of these stems from the fact that professional men, by the very nature of their work, have a natural tendency to operate more or less independently, with the result that an organization of professional men is apt to drift in the direction of a loose federation of individual practitioners, as opposed to the proper objective of becoming an integrated firm. The second of the differentiating factors, while somewhat related to the first, is sufficiently significant to be recognized and identified separately. This is the ever-present problem of capturing and recording the experience of the various professional men within the organization in such a way that it will be available to the entire organization—present and future. Unless these important day-to-day professional experiences are effectively recorded for the future use of the other professional personnel, they will be lost when the individual who obtained the experience leaves the organization, either through retirement or for other reasons. When a person leaves, he takes with him the benefit of his years of experience, and the younger personnel following must, in their own right, build up a new storehouse of experience. Thus, the fund of knowledge tends to remain static because it is geared to individuals rather than to the organization as a whole.

A professional firm is able to pass on to its clients the benefits which should accrue from being served by a large, diversified organization only if its collective experience is stored in such a way as to be readily available for all people to use. Thus, early in the firm's history it became apparent to the management that, in order to assure Arthur Andersen & Co. a vigorous growth commensurate with the growth of the economy, we must focus ever-increasing attention on the critical problem of communication. It was recognized that the future success of the firm would depend to a considerable extent on how well this critical problem was handled.

THE SUBJECT FILE

The idea of establishing a Subject File, identical files to be maintained in all of our offices, was discussed in the late 1930's and started in 1941. It was the brain child of Leonard Spacek, who recognized the vital importance of bringing together and filing in an orderly manner the wealth of pertinent material that was being accumulated. The Subject File as it exists today, with its great volume of accounting data and experience painstakingly classified and indexed to facilitate ready reference, is a living monument to the vision and the perseverance of Mr. Spacek.

The primary objectives in establishing the Subject File were to create—

1. A historical record of the development of the accounting principles and auditing standards recognized by the accounting profession.

2. A medium for assembling and making available to the entire organization the experiences of everyone connected with the firm with respect to accounting and auditing problems and statement presentation. It is the responsibility of each partner to write up and submit his pertinent cases for the Subject File.

3. A medium for bringing together current material of value for training or reference purposes and for making it available to every office of the firm.

What it meant in practical terms was that whenever any member of our professional organization encountered a technical problem new to him, he had ready access to the accumulated experience of the whole firm on that particular problem. Further, it was readily apparent that this new idea could give tremendous support to our concept of speaking with one voice. The file grew rather slowly during the early years of its use. The impetus for its substantial development came when its true value became apparent to all of the partners.

The current subject file index lists over 50,000 separate items and more than 100,000 additional cross-indexings. Thirteen persons in our worldwide headquarters now devote their full time to the operations of the file. We believe that no other professional organization in the world has anything that can match this. Items dated prior to 1972 have been put on microfilm and we are currently in the process of filming the material through 1973. Possible new techniques for recording, storing, indexing and retrieving are constantly being studied.

THE ARTHUR ANDERSEN CHRONICLE

Although it is believed that the adoption and installation of the Subject File was the most important single step taken with respect to the communication problem, there are a number of other ideas that have been adopted in our efforts to improve communication within the firm. One of these is our quarterly publication, *The Chronicle*.

The first issue of *The Chronicle* was published in October, 1940. During the period of more than three decades that have elapsed since then, it has grown in stature and has been eminently successful in promoting the fundamental idea of one voice and one firm.

THE PEOPLE OF ARTHUR ANDERSEN & CO.

In December, 1973, the first issue of a new quarterly publication called *The PEOPLE of Arthur Andersen & Co.* was released. This publication will incorporate the articles and news-type items of a more personal nature heretofore included in *The Chronicle,* and the latter will now be devoted largely to professional practice matters, financial and tax reporting changes, and current developments in computer and other systems technology. The first issue of *The Chronicle* under its new format will appear in 1974.

INTEROFFICE COMMUNICATION

Beginning in the middle 1940's, every U. S. office was connected with every other U. S. office by the means of teletype (TWX). This was done to assure that offices would communicate and check freely with each other on matters that might not seem to justify a long-distance telephone call. Furthermore, the written record of the communication minimizes the possibility of misinterpreting decisions or conclusions and eliminates the cost, incident to telephone calls, of writing subsequent file memorandums. This emphasis on interoffice communication has proved very useful.

In 1962, a Telex system was substituted for the TWX in order that the overseas offices could be a part of the direct wire network. As soon as facsimile transmission (DEX) was commercially available, we equipped all offices in the United States and Canada with this means of duplicating a page of written material over telephone lines in a matter of minutes.

FIRM-WIDE MEETINGS

One means that has been used extensively in our effort to cope with the problem of communication is the firm-wide meeting. These meetings, organized for the most part by functions or industries, furnish a forum for exchanging information and ideas. Also, we attempt, through these meetings, to establish and maintain the personal relationships that are so important to the esprit de corps of any organization, particularly a professional service organization.

ANNUAL PARTNERS' MEETING

Since inception, the firm has held an annual partners' meeting for the purpose of transacting necessary partnership business. However, it is also used for discussions among partners about our worldwide clients, about world accounting standards, about transfers of people and a variety of other administrative and professional practice matters. In 1964, the Chairman's Dinner was instituted as a part of the meeting, so that husbands and wives can meet and talk with others from our worldwide organization.

The annual partners' meeting was held in Chicago until 1972, when the location was Washington, D. C., returning to Chicago for the 1973 meeting. In 1974, the meeting will be held in New York City. (See pages 18, 40 and 41 for photographs of annual partners' meetings in 1930, 1953 and 1973 respectively.)

THE EXECUTIVE TEAM

A new communication device of relatively recent origin is a book called *The Executive Team,* first published in 1960. This book was conceived by Leonard Spacek as a means of introducing each member of our executive group and his family to the entire organization. It contains a picture of each partner and each manager and his family with an accompanying synopsis of their background and interests. It has proved to be surprisingly helpful in maintaining the personal nature of our organization in spite of its growing size.

ANNUAL REPORT TO OUR WORLDWIDE ORGANIZATION

The latest addition to our program for communication within our organization was the issuance of our first annual report to our worldwide organization for the year ended March 31, 1973. This was not only a "first" for Arthur Andersen & Co. but it was a "first" for the profession. Printed in five languages (English, French, German, Italian and Spanish) it gave every person in our worldwide organization an intimate look at our activities for the year and our financial results. In his introductory paragraph, Mr. Kapnick commented as follows:

> *"On December 1, 1973, Arthur Andersen & Co. will celebrate its sixtieth anniversary. In recognition of the growing size and complexities of our worldwide organization and the desirability of communicating directly to each of you our objectives, accomplishments, opportunities, concerns and financial results, we have decided to issue this—our first—annual report. We take this step of disclosure in the interest of developing an even closer relationship between the partners and all the other men and women of our worldwide organization. Today each member of our organization must be completely informed about significant aspects of our operations if we are to achieve the cohesiveness required to maintain our independence, reputation and professional competence."*

It is not easy to "hide a light under a bushel" and the word that we had issued an annual report to our organization was soon out in the profession. Although distribution of the report was initially restricted to our own people, a limited number of copies were made available to others on request and the report received widespread interest and approval outside the firm. This proved to be another milestone event in the last of the firm's first sixty years.

Our First Annual Report

CENTRAL CONTROL OF PERSONNEL, RECRUITING AND TRAINING

It has been accepted as axiomatic that the standardization of personnel policies, recruiting procedures and training programs throughout the world has contributed in a major way to the maintenance of our one-firm concept. Through the centralized control and direction of these functions we have been able to maintain an enviable record over the years for attracting outstanding young men and women and for providing them with the training necessary to take advantage of the opportunities offered by the firm for personal growth and professional achievement. This area of our operation has played such an important part in our history that an entire chapter (Chapter Eleven—"The Development of People") is being devoted to it.

SPECIALIZED COMPETENCE BY INDUSTRY

During the decade of 1931-1940, Mr. Andersen came to the conclusion that the sum total of accounting knowledge was beyond the intellectual comprehension of any one man, particularly in light of the growing size and complexity of many business enterprises. If the firm was to render expert service in all of the wide fields of industry and finance, it was necessary that certain men who were experienced in particular lines of business should concentrate more intensively on those lines and should be known throughout the firm as specialists in their particular industries. His first step was to assign to men possessing special experience the task of compiling detailed information, in the form of Industry Reference Binders, on selected types of businesses, such as finance companies, department stores, airlines and the lumber industry. These were the forerunners of our present-day Industry Reference Binders—much less complete and sophisticated and for only a handful of industries, but it was a beginning. As time went on, the list was expanded to include many other industries such as banking and finance, farms and ranches, food products, furniture, insurance, machine tools, mining, oil and gas, paper, real estate, regulated industries, shipping and textiles.

Eventually, individual partners with extensive experience in a particular industry were selected to head the respective industry groups and each such partner (usually an audit partner) was given the responsibility for correlating all the work of the firm in his assigned industry, for advancing the level of the firm's competence in that industry, for keeping all members of the industry group informed as to the latest industry developments and for assisting engagement partners throughout the firm in handling specific industry problems. Designated partners from our tax and administrative services divisions were also assigned to assist these respective industry heads in order to involve all of our disciplines in the industry approach. With increasing frequency, the joint endeavors of audit, tax and administrative services personnel have contributed to important breakthroughs in solving industry problems.

Another important result of the industry program is that any office in the firm is able to make available promptly to our clients in that office the worldwide experience and competence of the firm in any given industry. Qualified industry specialists are always available for short or long periods to assist any office which has a need for industry competence not yet developed locally.

More recently, we have taken steps to put our various industry categories into the following major groups, with a managing partner in charge of each respective group:

Consumer Goods, Business and Personal Services
Financial Services
Government Services
Natural Resources
Regulated Industries

The management of the firm is dedicated to a further expansion of our industry competence program as one of the keys to the continuing development of the quality of our service to clients.

PRACTICE DIRECTORS

The designation of practice directors in all three divisions of our practice came as a more recent development in response to our growing size. The title of practice director first came into official use in 1970 as a part of the new organization plan (see Chapter Eight), but the function was not new. The heads of the three divisions had always been responsible for the quality of our practice in each of their respective areas and had selected others to assist them. As both the number of offices and the number of clients grew, it became impossible for a mere handful of people to carry out this function, and the concept of practice directors was adopted. These men are located throughout the world with responsibility for designated geographical areas, and they provide the means for a fast response and consistent approach to the understanding and handling of our clients' problems. In 1973, there were 36 practice directors operating in the three divisions as follows:

Audit	7
Taxes	12
Administrative Services	17
TOTAL	36

Each practice director reports directly to the head of his division who is a vice chairman of the firm. The work of the practice directors is, of course, only one part of our many faceted program of quality control.

COPING WITH NEW PATTERNS OF LITIGATION

The importance of the firm's policy, through all of its existence, of maintaining the highest standards of professional work has been further underscored by the significant increase during the last decade in the amount of litigation involving the public accounting profession. This has been especially aggravated by the so-called class action suits of recent years.

Our own position in this area was set forth in our March 31, 1973 annual report to our worldwide organization, as follows:

"The legal responsibilities of officers, directors, lawyers, investment bankers and auditors are constantly changing. During the past decade, litigation involving our profession has shown a dramatic increase in the United States. This type of litigation has been a way of life with many large corporations for a number of years, but it is new to the accounting profession and to our organization.

"In the United States many companies which by their very nature are developmental, promotional and of the venture capital type have gone to the public security markets for equity or debt capital. Our involvement with many companies of this type is initiated by clients or directors of clients of long standing. In a private enterprise system a substantial number of companies that begin as new ventures are likely to fail. We have no crystal ball to tell which will succeed and which will fail, and we do not

*believe it is in the public interest for auditing firms with estab-
lished reputations to decline these engagements.*

*"In addition, established companies occasionally encounter
serious financial difficulties. As auditors, we are well aware of
these conditions and attempt to respond with thoughtful consideration of each important accounting and auditing issue.
Nevertheless, if these clients cannot overcome their difficulties,
we inevitably will be a legal target for those who seek to salvage
something from their investment or creditor position.*

*"We do not believe that it has ever been the basic intent in
appointing auditors to have them guarantee investors or creditors
against losses. A substantial amount of our litigation is in these
areas.*

*"We recognize that control over our practice is paramount.
In the few instances where we determined that our work did not
meet our standards, we quickly resolved the issues in an appropriate manner. But even in these circumstances, in today's environment, we usually receive wide publicity which places an oc-
casional problem completely out of context. As of March 31,
1973, litigation involving 28 clients or former clients was pending.
We are informed that more than 500 companies have litigation
or claims in process involving auditors at the present time."*

The number of twenty-eight must be viewed in the light of the fact
that the firm has over fifty thousand clients and that these cases had arisen
over a period of several years.

A particularly vexing piece of litigation deserving special mention has
been the Four Seasons Nursing Centers of America, Inc., a case in which
two of our partners and one of our managers were involved in a criminal
trial commencing at the close of 1973. The case related to our auditors'
opinion covering the company's 1968 and 1969 financial statements. We
had required this client to make substantial downward adjustments of
earnings in its financial statements before our engagement was completed
and we were confident that our personnel had performed their work with
complete independence and objectivity and with appropriate professional
skill. The trial was concluded in February, 1974, and the verdict by the

jury on February 7, 1974, was a vindication of our personnel. The following three paragraphs were contained in Mr. Kapnick's release to the press after the verdict:

> *"The government has failed to prove its case against any of the Arthur Andersen & Co. personnel involved in the Four Seasons trial in Oklahoma City. The verdict by the jury on February 7, 1974, acquitted Edward Bolka, a partner, and Jimmie Madole, a manager, of all charges alleged by the government. The jury was divided 9 to 3 in favor of acquittal of Kenneth Wahrman, a partner, and a mistrial was declared as to Mr. Wahrman. Mr. Wahrman had previously successfully passed a polygraph test which the government elected to ignore.*

> *"All the partners of Arthur Andersen & Co. have the utmost respect for these men and appreciation for the tremendous sacrifice that has been made by them and their families in defending themselves and our firm against the charges asserted by the government. The trial conducted in the U. S. District Court for the Western District of Oklahoma extended over a period of ten weeks. The government alleged that the Arthur Andersen auditors had been involved in a conspiracy with others, including certain Four Seasons officers and directors, to commit fraud in approving the financial statements of the company for the fiscal years 1968 and 1969, knowing that such statements included false, fictitious, and nonexistent construction costs. No credible evidence was presented to support these allegations.*

> *"This verdict is a significant victory for our personnel and confirms our firm's position that the audits involved were proper and were conducted in a professional manner. The verdict of the jury also rejects the charges by the Securities and Exchange Commission, including the testimony for the government by its accountants, that the audits were not proper and did not support our firm's opinion with respect to the financial statements."*

It is hoped that the firm's aggressive action in this and other cases will inspire others in the profession to join in vigorous action against unjustified claims to the end that third parties will be discouraged from instituting capricious and unwarranted suits against members of the profession. In the meantime, we will make every effort to maintain the highest possible quality standards in our professional practice.

CHAPTER ELEVEN

The Development of People

EARLY EMPHASIS ON COLLEGE TRAINING

Early in his practice, Arthur Andersen became convinced that the future of his firm would depend on his ability to surround himself with able young people. He wanted college graduates who not only had an interest in accounting but who also had the ability to think for themselves. At first, as a Professor and Head of the Accounting Department at Northwestern University, he did his own recruiting primarily from among the students in his classes. Later, as the organization grew, and he no longer had a teaching relationship with Northwestern University, he also looked to other universities as a source of new material. One of the first of these was the University of Illinois, which already had a well-developed accounting curriculum and was near at hand. During the earlier years of the firm, graduates of these two universities constituted a significant part of the organization.

For the first twenty years, most of the recruiting was done by the partners themselves, with the assistance of J. O. Johnson, who at that time was office manager in Chicago. (He was later to become the partner in charge of the firm's small business practice.)

THE NEW POSITION OF DIRECTOR OF PERSONNEL

A major forward step in the firm's recruiting program was taken in 1938, when Vilas Johnson was appointed director of personnel for the firm. Mr. Johnson, Mr. Andersen's son-in-law, was a gifted recruiter and over the years developed a strong relationship with the leading universities and colleges throughout the United States. For many years, he personally carried out our recruiting, assisted by representatives of the respective offices.

SOLVING THE PROBLEM OF PEAK SEASON REQUIREMENTS

While most of our permanent professional personnel in the earlier years came from colleges and universities, it was a general practice of public accounting firms prior to World War II to hire large numbers of temporary staff in the late fall and winter months to cover their peak season requirements. Arthur Andersen & Co. was no exception to this practice. The great preponderance of companies ended their business years on December 31 and this, along with other factors, produced such a high peaking in the "busy season" that it seemed impossible to carry for the full year enough staff to meet peak needs.

These temporary employees constituted a more stable group than might first appear. A considerable number of them came back year after year and had seasonal jobs to keep them employed for the remainder of the year—pursers on lake steamers, accountants from summer camps, farmers with an accounting background, and others. Even university graduates sometimes had to serve for a season or two on a temporary basis before being added to the permanent staff. Much of the work at that level was fairly routine and, when carefully supervised, did not require a major degree of professional expertise.

World War II indirectly changed much of that. When the available supply of temporary manpower for the busy season began to be depleted, it became necessary to seek alternative ways of handling the work. For example, careful study and experimentation proved that a large part of the more routine audit work could be carried out satisfactorily in the summer and fall as "preliminary work." Clients helped to ease their own peak-load problems as well as that of the auditors by taking their physical inventories a month or more prior to December 31. Some companies were agreeable to changing their fiscal year end from December 31 to a more natural business year. Actually, for a great many companies, the end of the calendar year was not the best time to close their books and they found it advantageous to their own purposes to close their accounts when their inventories and receivables were at a low point.

With new and imaginative approaches, the January and February peak-load problem, although far from being eliminated, was considerably reduced. It then became practicable to take the more professional view that the maintenance of an adequate public accounting staff should not be dependent on the hiring of temporary personnel, but that the staff should be built and maintained on a permanent basis. We believe that our firm was one of the leaders in this move toward a more professional status for the staff accountant.

NEW EMPHASIS ON RECRUITING

It is obvious that a public accounting firm can give better service to its clients if its staff is composed entirely of permanent people who have prepared themselves for a career in public accounting. However, the effect of this trend away from the use of temporary staff, coinciding as it did with the rapid expansion of the practice of public accounting firms after the war, very quickly brought into focus the fact that none of the firms had enough personnel to meet the increasing demands of the business world. The situation was particularly acute in the large firms. The annual supply of college graduates with accounting majors was, and still is, inadequate to meet all of the needs of public accounting and industry. It quickly became apparent that if our firm was to succeed in hiring enough capable graduates to meet our over-all requirements, it would be necessary to change our approach to our recruiting. We needed to expand our coverage of colleges and universities and to devote more time to our recruiting activities. Obviously, it no longer would be practical for Vilas Johnson to continue his round of personal campus visits and this he delegated to the individual offices. At the same time, a program was designed for the centralized control of all our recruiting activities. The needs of each office were meshed with those of the other offices. Recruiting methods were studied and the best were adopted by all. The work of each office was monitored carefully to assure that uniform recruiting practices were being followed and high quality standards for entrance into the organization uniformly maintained.

The new approach proved to be a sound one, and it formed the foundation for our recruiting for the years ahead when our search for qualified graduates would reach proportions not yet dreamed of. Our recruiting program continues to be an all-offices effort coordinated centrally in World Headquarters. Growing needs and increasingly intense competition for qualified college graduates have caused us to devote more and more time and resources to recruiting. In recent years we have held seminars and training sessions for our recruiters in Australia, Europe, South America and the United States. Our training now includes video tape recordings of live interviews to permit our recruiters to see and hear themselves and to help them improve their interviewing techniques.

STANDARDIZATION OF PERSONNEL POLICIES

Also, as the number of our offices began to grow, the need for a further standardization of our personnel policies became more apparent. It was important for the firm to have uniform personnel policies that would be followed consistently in all offices and for our people everywhere to believe in the fairness of these policies. The merits of this approach became even more apparent as we grew into a worldwide organization.

Eventually, our personnel policies were written out in considerable detail and printed in a personnel reference binder which discussed, among other things, the organization and objectives of the firm, its personnel and operating policies and its training methods. This binder has continued to be updated to meet changing times.

We have long emphasized our merit approach to advancement, and the firm's practice of gearing an employee's salary to the rate which can be billed for his services was adopted in the late 1930's. Another major policy was that the opportunity for advancement was as good in one office as another. An employee's opportunity is firm-wide, not merely in his own office.

OUR PERSONNEL ACTIVITIES EXPAND

In 1945, our personnel group in Chicago was further strengthened through the addition of a young man who, for the preceding five years, had been working in the Boston office on a part-time basis while serving as a member of the faculty of Harvard's Graduate School of Business Administration. Prior to 1940, he had been on the staff of our New York office for four years. Richard Claire thus brought to his new responsibilities a rich background of academic and professional experience and with his outstanding personal qualities he was an instant success. He was admitted to partnership in 1947 and later he succeeded Vilas Johnson as director of personnel when Mr. Johnson retired from the firm in 1952.

Mr. Claire was an early advocate of the program of internships for university students interested in careers in public accounting, and it is generally acknowledged that primarily through his efforts, internship programs were established in many universities throughout the world. He established the Arthur Andersen & Co. Fellowship Program for Doctoral Candidates to enable prospective accounting teachers to complete their doctoral dissertations undisturbed by financial pressures. Other products of his efforts were our program for matching contributions for the financial support of colleges and universities and our faculty residences in public accounting for accounting teachers.

In 1966, Mr. Claire was succeeded by Claude Rodgers as director of personnel and recruiting, and for the next three years, until his untimely death in 1969 at the age of 62, Mr. Claire devoted his efforts primarily to our recruiting program.

In 1965, our recruiting activities were extended to the country's predominantly black universities. Again, the firm was a leader in that we were the first of the large public accounting firms to recruit at these universities. Initially, the campus interviews were carried out by Mr. Claire, himself, because he wanted to make certain that the interviews were conducted on exactly the same basis as at the other universities where we were already recruiting. In a few years, however, the progress in civil rights throughout the United States had reached a point where special treatment for the predominantly black universities was no longer necessary or desirable, and full recruiting activities were taken over thereafter by the local offices.

For many years, the firm employed only men for its professional staff but in more recent years, in keeping with the times, both men and women have been recruited on an equal basis.

We are committed to the principle of assisting all people who are willing to work for our objectives to achieve the highest use of their talents. Every effort is made to make sure that each person who is qualified progresses as rapidly as possible regardless of race, color or sex.

In 1958, the firm produced its first recruiting brochure; in subsequent years, our recruiting brochures were considerably expanded and refined. In 1973, separate editions were produced in 11 geographical areas of the world involving five different languages.

Examples of Recruiting Brochures
(Note the Japanese Edition)

While statistics cannot tell the whole story, some idea of the importance of our recruiting activities may be gleaned from these figures. We now recruit from over 750 colleges and universities in 27 countries. In 1973, in the U.S. alone, we conducted over 16,000 campus interviews and over 4,000 students were invited to an Arthur Andersen & Co. office for further in-depth interviews. On a worldwide basis we employed 2,349 college and university recruits of whom 683 were in non-U.S. countries.

The uniformly high quality of our personnel throughout the world today is, in itself, a tribute to the outstanding success of our recruiting efforts through the years and of our training program, which also has been a key instrument in our development of people.

TRAINING—A HIGH PRIORITY FROM THE BEGINNING

Training has always had a high priority in the firm. Arthur Andersen's interest in teaching carried over into his new organization and he was always sharing his knowledge and experience with the younger members. At that time, it was traditional for all public accounting firms to rely heavily on on-the-job training as a means of developing and training their staff. Certainly no one can argue that this method had not been successful from the standpoint of the end product, a thoroughly trained staff person, and it still is one of the mainstays of our training efforts. However, our problem was that this was much too slow a process if the firm was to keep pace with the growth that was being thrust upon it.

THE FIRMWIDE AUDIT STAFF TRAINING SCHOOLS FOR NEW PERSONNEL

During the latter part of the 1930's, it became evident that some formal training mechanism was needed to bridge the gap between the theoretical accounting training of the campus and the working knowledge of accounting and auditing which must be acquired as rapidly as possible by the new recruit.

This could have been done by holding training schools in each of our offices or in four or five sections of the country, but our concept of "speaking with one voice" seemed to indicate that we should strive for uniformity of training by holding a central school in Chicago.

The first school was held during the month of August, 1940, under the direction of Vilas Johnson and Kenneth M. Montgomery. Affectionately known as "Monty Tech," it was attended by thirty-five recent graduates who had been employed by the various offices of the firm from twenty-three colleges and universities, ranging all the way from Harvard on the east coast to Stanford on the west coast.

The principal objective of our training school was to acquaint the new recruits with our approach to auditing and to give them some practical experience in the making of an audit. Our program eventually came to be based on an audit practice case of a typical medium-sized manufacturing company, which we prepared. All of the basic records of the company necessary for an audit are reproduced for each student, and each set contains memorandums on the history, business, accounting procedures and internal control of the company, and an audit program in sufficient detail to guide the student in making the audit.

Before each phase of the practice case is worked, there is a discussion, supported by audio tapes and workbooks, on the particular accounts involved and our objectives in planning the work to be done in auditing these accounts. The students then proceed to make that portion of the audit which has just been discussed, not in a vacuum, but with such help as they may need from the experienced faculty recruited from our organization. Small group critiques are then conducted in which the students review their papers in a manner similar to that which would be followed by the senior in actual practice.

Throughout the school, various partners speak to the group on such subjects as the organization of the firm, professional ethics and conduct, and the position of the firm on various current accounting questions.

Upon completion of the school, an evaluation is made of the performance of each student and points of strength and weakness are noted. These evaluations form the basis for the continuing training and counseling of the individuals as they begin actual auditing engagements.

We have found this method of training to be highly effective. It has, of course, been refined considerably over the years under the direction of Richard Claire and, later, of Carl J. Bohne, Jr., who was elected to partnership in 1956 and given partnership responsibility for training in recognition of the growing importance of this activity in the firm.

As the number of new employees each year increased, it became necessary to increase the number of identical sessions of the school. They now last approximately three weeks and are held at different times of the year and in centrally located cities around the world. Three days of the three weeks' instruction are conducted in the local offices using video tape demonstrations and other centrally prepared materials. In 1973, 14 schools in five countries were attended by about 2,225 persons. We are satisfied that these schools have been very effective in shortening the period that the newly hired public accountant has to spend as a staff accountant in learning the techniques of auditing. Friendships formed in these schools, many of an international scope, have also been a strong cohesive force in the firm.

Firmwide schools are also conducted in income taxes and in administrative services. In the latter area, alone, we currently offer twenty firm-wide courses a year which have been specially designed to meet the rapidly changing technology in the administrative services field.

Numerous training programs have been devised to accelerate the development of our people at all stages of their professional growth. One of these is the industry competence program in which training schools are developed and conducted with the primary objective of training selected individuals in depth in each of the principal industries. We have concluded that substantive knowledge and understanding of an industry, its distinctive characteristics and its problems, afford the only sound foundation for the effective discharge of any assignment, whether it be in the area of audit, taxes or administrative services.

Needless to say, these formalized training programs are costly in terms of direct dollar outlay and in terms of the time of the personnel involved in the training activity. Over a period of time, our training costs have amounted each year to about 6% of our annual fees, but the firm is convinced that they are essential to the development of our professional staff at a rate rapid enough to keep pace with the growth and increasing complexity of our practice.

OUR CENTER FOR PROFESSIONAL DEVELOPMENT

Inasmuch as an important part of our training effort is accomplished on a centralized basis, a decision was made in 1970 to purchase a training facility in St. Charles, Illinois, on a fifty-five acre tract forty-five miles from downtown Chicago. This facility, which was originally built to house a small resident college, has been named our Center for Professional Development. With the recent completion of further additions to the buildings, living accommodations are now available for approximately 650 people. Mr. Bohne, as director of training, with headquarters at the Center, is assisted by four other partners and two managers on a full-time basis. Partners, managers and staff come to this center from all parts of the world and last year our training activities at this facility alone amounted to approximately 70,000 training days.

A television studio installed at the Center has enabled us to prepare video training tapes (in color) on cassettes for use in all of our offices. This studio and many of our video tape techniques were developed under the leadership of its present director, Harry E. Paney. We can thus bring current professional developments more quickly and expertly to all our personnel. Further, this new method enables us to concentrate more of our training at our local office level and reduces instruction preparation time at both the local and central levels. It also permits our professional personnel to use the video tape lectures and demonstrations at times convenient to them.

We believe that we have one of the best in-house training programs in the world today. From the beginning, an important element in the success of our program has been the use of line personnel as faculty in all of our schools. In addition to its contribution to the building of our professional competence, our training program has been an important factor in maintaining our one-firm concept and our policy of speaking with one voice.

The Arthur Andersen & Co. Center for Professional Development at St. Charles, Illinois. The new residence hall addition is seen at the lower right, and construction in progress for the new Leonard Spacek Auditorium (dotted lines) upper center.

OUR SOCIAL RESPONSIBILITIES

Throughout its history, the firm has encouraged participation by all of our people in professional and community activities. We are deeply committed to meeting our responsibilities in these areas in each country where we practice, and the firm, itself, has contributed substantial sums of money and professional time annually to various programs.

Some of our activities in the professional field are referred to in Chapter Twelve. In the areas of community and social service as well as in the professional field, many of our men and women, particularly at the partner and manager level, have distinguished themselves as leaders in many and varied activities. We are indeed proud of the contributions that our people around the world have made to the betterment of their respective communities and to the progress of mankind.

CHAPTER TWELVE

Leadership in the Profession

From its inception, the Firm has been intensely interested in the use-fulness and fairness of accounting and financial reporting. Further, it has always taken the position that it has an important responsibility to the public and the accounting profession to make every possible effort to achieve progress in the development of sound accounting principles and reporting standards.

The creation of the Committee on Technique in 1929 (see Chapter Ten) established an effective vehicle within the firm for the development and codification of accounting and auditing policies. As this committee evolved into the Committee on Accounting Principles and Auditing Procedures, its research efforts were expanded and its members began to take an increasingly active part in the broader arena of the profession as a whole. Many partners and managers were also becoming involved in the affairs of state societies and on committees of the American Institute of Certified Public Accountants. But it was not until the 1950's that the full impact of the firm's participation in the profession began to manifest itself under the dynamic leadership of Leonard Spacek.

THE FIRM SPEAKS OUT

By the 1950's, Mr. Spacek had become convinced that the profession was floundering in the area of accounting principles. The Institute's principal accounting research body, the Committee on Accounting Procedures, had been issuing opinions for a considerable number of years but had been unable to develop a consistent, logical body of theory or to deal effectively with some of the more difficult problems. In his view, one of its principal faults was that it had failed to define the objectives of accounting as a proper background for its consideration of individual problems. Instead of developing guidelines or principles based upon logic and reasoned consideration, it had become overly absorbed in detailed rule making.

Mr. Spacek believed that the overriding objective of accounting was the presentation of financial information which would be "fair" to all segments of society who were the users of the information, e.g., stockholders, management, labor, consumers, creditors and government. In an article entitled "Challenge to Public Accounting" appearing in the May-June, 1958, issue of the *Harvard Business Review* he stated it this way:

> *"Consumers, business, and labor must have an independent professional body to establish the accounting principles by which the profits used in negotiating prices and wages and in making investment decisions are determined. These principles must be determined as independently of business influence as of the influence of labor and consumers.*

> *"When accounting principles are determined in a manner that is fair to each of the conflicting interests, consumers can determine from the reports to the public whether the prices they pay for the products result in fair wages and a fair return on capital. Different groups may argue as to how the profits are to be distributed, but what the profits are should not be subject to confusion and controversy. Until objective standards of accounting are established, adopted by the profession, and explained concisely to the public, corporate reports will continue to be suspect to all. Certainly we do not want rigid regulations. We want all the flexibility needed so that each company can report as accurately as possible on its own situation. But we also want better standards of what is right and what is wrong to govern the choice of alternative methods of reporting costs and income."*

In addition to the underlying objective of fairness, it was mandatory, in Mr. Spacek's view, that a better procedure be developed for documenting the reasons for the adoption of any particular accounting principle so that both the public and the profession could understand the basis of its formulation and the reasons for its acceptance.

Inasmuch as the accounting profession constituted one of the most important contributors to the decision-making process in our democratic system, he felt impelled to exert every personal effort to see that the profession lived up to this responsibility. Having been unsuccessful in his efforts to change the direction of the profession by working from within, he eventually decided to take his case to the public.

On February 12, 1957, in an address before the Milwaukee Control of the Controllers Institute of America, he expressed his first major public criticism of the work of the Committee on Accounting Procedures. For the next sixteen years until his retirement in 1973, in speech after speech (over 200 of them), his voice was raised to challenge the status quo and to offer both criticism and creative suggestions.

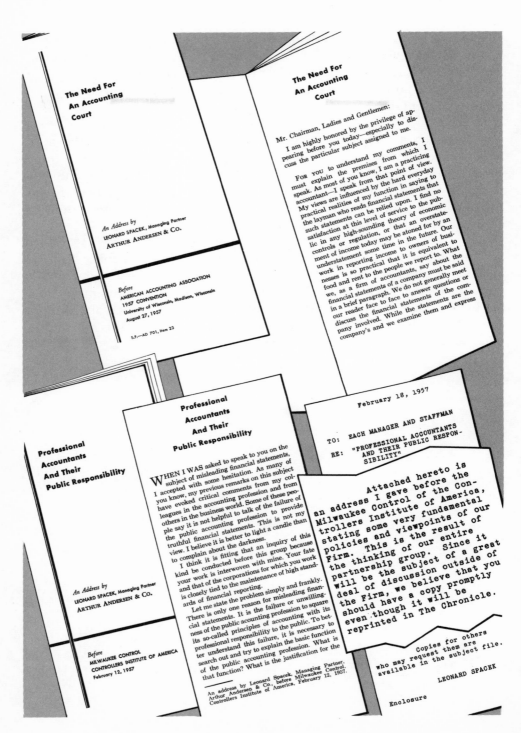

The Need For An Accounting Court

An Address by
LEONARD SPACEK, Managing Partner
ARTHUR ANDERSEN & CO.

Before
AMERICAN ACCOUNTING ASSOCIATION
1957 CONVENTION
University of Wisconsin, Madison, Wisconsin
August 27, 1957

S.F.—AD 701, Item 23

The Need For An Accounting Court

Mr. Chairman, Ladies and Gentlemen:

I am highly honored by the privilege of appearing before you today—especially to discuss the particular subject assigned to me.

FOR YOU to understand my comments, I must explain the premises from which I speak. As most of you know, I am a practicing accountant—I speak from that point of view. My views are influenced by the hard everyday practical realities of my function in saying to the layman who reads financial statements that such statements can be relied upon. I find no satisfaction at this level of service to the public in any high-sounding theory of economic controls or regulation, or that an overstatement of income today may be atoned for by an understatement some time in the future. Our work in reporting income to owners of businesses is so practical that it is equivalent to food and rent to the people we report to. What we, as a firm of accountants, say about the financial statements of a company must be said in a brief paragraph. We do not generally meet our reader face to face to answer questions or discuss the financial statements of the company involved. While the statements are the company's and we examine them and express

Professional Accountants And Their Public Responsibility

WHEN I WAS asked to speak to you on the subject of misleading financial statements, I accepted with some hesitation. As many of you know, my previous remarks on this subject have evoked critical comments from my colleagues in the accounting profession and from others in the business world. Some of these people say it is not helpful to talk of the failure of the public accounting profession to provide truthful financial statements. This is not my view. I believe it is better to light a candle than to complain about the darkness.

I think it is fitting that an inquiry of this kind be conducted before this group because your work is interwoven with mine. Your fate and that of the corporations for which you work is closely tied to the maintenance of high standards of financial reporting.

Let me state the problem simply and frankly. There is only one reason for misleading financial statements. It is the failure or unwillingness of the public accounting profession to square its so-called principles of accounting with its professional responsibility to the public. To better understand this failure, it is necessary to search out and try to explain the basic function of the public accounting profession. What is that function? What is the justification for the

An address by Leonard Spacek, Managing Partner, Arthur Andersen & Co., before Milwaukee Control, Controllers Institute of America, February 12, 1957.

Professional Accountants And Their Public Responsibility

An Address by
LEONARD SPACEK, Managing Partner
ARTHUR ANDERSEN & CO.

Before
MILWAUKEE CONTROL
CONTROLLERS INSTITUTE OF AMERICA
February 12, 1957

February 18, 1957

TO: EACH MANAGER AND STAFFMAN

RE: "PROFESSIONAL ACCOUNTANTS AND THEIR PUBLIC RESPONSIBILITY"

Attached hereto is an address I gave before the Milwaukee Control of the Controllers Institute of America, stating some very fundamental policies and viewpoints of our Firm. This is the result of the thinking of our entire partnership group. Since it will be the subject of a great deal of discussion outside of the Firm, we believe that you should have a copy promptly even though it will be reprinted in The Chronicle.

Copies for others who may request them are available in the subject file.

LEONARD SPACEK

Enclosure

As could be expected, Mr. Spacek was subjected to continuing criticism, and even a degree of personal abuse, by some members of the profession. A few months after his Milwaukee address, a committee was appointed by the American Institute of Certified Public Accountants to investigate his criticisms and to determine what disciplinary action, if any, should be taken. The committee's report to the Council of the Institute was hotly debated and thanks in part to the oratorical talent of Richard Claire, who was then a member of the Council, it was defeated. Mr. Spacek continued to stand his ground with courage and conviction and with the full support of the partnership still speaking with one voice. Eventually, growing numbers in the profession began to accept the merit of his position on many of the issues, and before his retirement he had the satisfaction of witnessing the adoption of ideas and programs that were in tune with the concepts he had espoused.

For example, at the 1957 convention of the American Accounting Association, Mr. Spacek formally proposed the establishment of a "court of accounting principles." He visualized this court as a professional tribunal to be established by the American Institute of Certified Public Accountants. It would set its own rules of procedure as to written briefs, arguments, etc. which would be similar to those followed in an appellate court; the Institute would adopt a charter amendment defining the criteria or objectives of accounting principles. The court would consist of three full-time members who would be elected for life with an age ceiling. Their salaries would be set by charter, preferably in relation to those of specified United States judges. The Institute would then be responsible for the costs of the court with a membership assessment on all practicing accountants and firms.

This concept of a court of accounting principles was designed primarily to overcome certain basic weaknesses in the structure and operation of the American Institute's Committee on Accounting Procedures. Briefly, these related particularly to (1) the lack of complete independence of members of the committee who served only on a voluntary, part-time basis and who retained their professional, business or academic ties; (2) the lack of an established procedure for receiving written briefs from all parties of interest; (3) the lack of documentation as to the basis for conclusions reached and the reasons why they were fair to all segments of society; and (4) the absence of an appropriate appeal procedure.

In December, 1957, four months after Mr. Spacek's formal proposal for a court of accounting principles, the American Institute appointed a committee, of which Mr. Spacek was a member, to consider a new approach to the formulation of accounting principles. The outgrowth of this study was the establishment of a new Accounting Principles Board, with a permanent research staff, to take the place of the old Committee on Accounting Procedures. In spite of considerable optimism over the Accounting Principles Board, it soon became apparent that the Board was subject to many of the same weaknesses as were inherent in its predecessor committee. Mr. Spacek revived his proposal for an accounting court which eventually began to attract a greater amount of support.

In November 1970, in a letter to Mr. Marshall Armstrong, president of the AICPA, Harvey Kapnick formally petitioned the AICPA to take prompt action in changing the organization and operations of the AICPA as they related to the establishment of accounting principles. Early in 1971, Mr. Armstrong called a conference of the senior leaders of the profession (including Mr. Kapnick) to consider how best to deal with these problems. As a result of recommendations made by this group, a seven-man study group (later called the Wheat Committee) was organized in March, 1971, which included significant representation from outside the profession. A year later, this committee submitted its recommendations to the AICPA's board of directors out of which the Financial Accounting Standards Board was created in 1973.

Thus, sixteen years after Mr. Spacek's original proposal, arrangements for an alternate approach were worked out under which a permanent organization to be called the Financial Accounting Standards Board was created to take the place of the Accounting Principles Board. The new Board is a completely independent body with seven full time members who are well compensated and who have disassociated themselves from their former professional or business ties. The Board is supported by contributions from members of the profession, and from business enterprises and foundations, and its operating procedures have incorporated a number of the basic suggestions advanced by Mr. Spacek in his proposal for the accounting court. The new board became operative in 1973 and everyone hopes for its success. This was but one example of Mr. Spacek's impact on the progress of the profession.

In an introduction to the second volume of Mr. Spacek's speeches, published in 1973 under the title *A Search for Fairness in Financial Reporting to the Public,* Harvey Kapnick wrote the following:

*"Many of the ideas which he (Leonard Spacek) has put for-
ward, although not immediately accepted, have stood the test of
fairness, with his partners, his supporters, and even his critics.
These ideas were the result of hours of thinking, discussion and
argument with his partners, who had great confidence in his
leadership. All of us have been proud of his forward thinking, his
willingness to break with the crowd when he thought he was right
and his ability to stand alone without arrogance or reliance on
position when he concluded that his answer to the issue was fair
to all involved.*

*"His pattern for the accounting profession and accounting
principles and his leadership in changing the course of the profession can be evaluated only by future generations. I am confident
that the ideas, thoughts and suggestions contained in these two
volumes will stand the test of time."*

While Mr. Spacek stood out above all the rest, many of the other
partners also played active roles in pressing for progress in the area of
accounting principles both in the U.S. and in other countries. Among
these were George R. Catlett, Norman Olson, Russell H. Morrison and other
members of our Committee on Accounting Principles and Auditing Procedures, as well as Albert J. Bows, Jr. and Harvey Kapnick. Some of the
speeches of Messrs. Catlett and Olson have recently been published in a
volume entitled *In Pursuit of Professional Goals* and a new volume of Mr.
Kapnick's speeches is being published under the title *In the Public
Interest.*

Our efforts in pressing for the development of sound accounting standards have not been confined to the USA. In Canada, Stephen Elliott served
from 1967 to 1972 as a member of the Accounting and Auditing Research
Committee of the Canadian Institute of Chartered Accountants, and was
the Committee's chairman from 1970 to 1972. Prior to 1970, he was chair-
man for one year of the Central Section of that committee. Since 1972,
Frank Barrett of the Dublin office has been a member of the combined
Accounting Standards Steering Committee of the Institute of Chartered
Accountants of England and Wales and of similar institutes of Scotland and
Ireland.

Thomas G. S. Sumner and others in our São Paulo and Rio de Janeiro
offices have demonstrated outstanding leadership in Brazil over the past

fifteen years in obtaining general acceptance of financial statements which have been adjusted for the effects of price-level changes. In Argentina, Santiago Lazzati of the Buenos Aires office is one of the recognized leaders in the accounting profession in that country. For many years, he has taught at the University of Buenos Aires and has had an important role in the Technical Institute of Public Accountants as a member of several committees including a committee on inflation accounting. In 1972, this Institute approved recommendations to establish recognition of price-level adjustments as a generally accepted accounting principle.

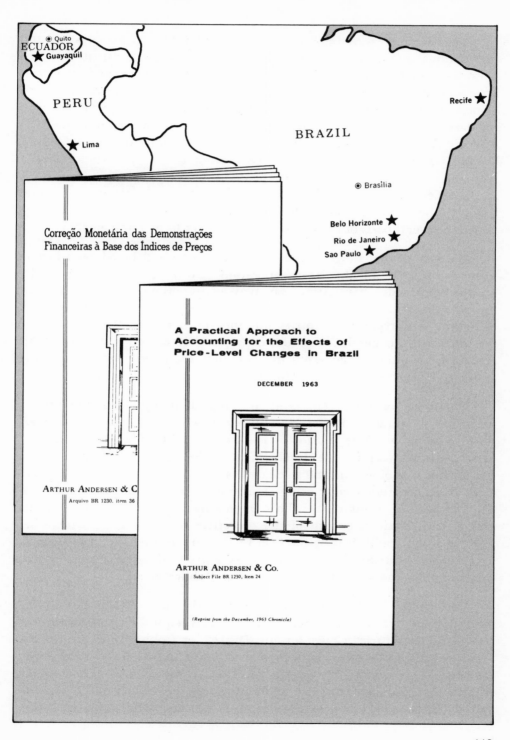

ECUADOR
Quito
Guayaquil

PERU

Lima

BRAZIL

Recife

Brasília

Belo Horizonte

Rio de Janeiro

Sao Paulo

Correção Monetária das Demonstrações
Financeiras à Base dos Índices de Preços

ARTHUR ANDERSEN & C
Arquivo BR 1230. item 36

A Practical Approach to
Accounting for the Effects of
Price-Level Changes in Brazil

DECEMBER 1963

ARTHUR ANDERSEN & CO.
Subject File BR 1230, Item 24

(Reprint from the December, 1963 Chronicle)

The ever-increasing importance of both international business and the transnational capital market, the evolution of the large multinational corporations and the experiences encountered in our own expanding worldwide operations have all highlighted the need for the development of a more comprehensive body of international accounting principles and standards. To this end, Mr. Kapnick in 1973 proposed the establishment of a World Accounting Council. This Council, which would be composed of leading business and professional men around the world, would have a permanent organization structure and would undertake the formulation and certification of international accounting standards. Although a tentative structure for the Council has been devised by Mr. Kapnick and discussed in several parts of the world, the plan is yet to be implemented.

We believe that world standards of accounting will be adopted in one form or another in the next generation and that the firm, with its unique worldwide organization, can play an important leadership role in this process. Such standards must not only cross the national boundaries of today's industrialized countries but they must also be appropriate for the third world countries. Further, if properly developed, they should cut across philosophies of government including those oriented toward the so-called "public enterprise" system of the communist bloc of countries.

Prompted by the urgent need for progress in this area, the firm is preparing a volume entitled *Accounting Standards for Business Enterprises Throughout The World* for issuance in 1974. This document will present a framework for the development of the worldwide policies of the firm in the area of accounting standards as well as a basis for the establishment of international accounting standards by the accounting profession and the business community. This framework, in turn, will have as its foundation a basic statement of the objectives of financial statements set forth in a book published by the firm in 1972 under the title of *Objectives of Financial Statements for Business Enterprises* discussed later in this chapter under the subject of "Professional Publications."

One of the most dramatic examples of the firm's leadership in the profession occurred as late as September, 1973, when it filed a motion in the United States District Court for the District of Columbia to enjoin the Securities and Exchange Commission from enforcing its Accounting Series Release No. 146 issued on August 24, 1973. This release related to the criteria for pooling-of-interests accounting where treasury stock was involved. In our view, that release was an unwarranted and improper action by the SEC on two counts. First, it changed the criteria for pooling-of-interests accounting without the prescribed requirement for prior exposure of the release and the acceptance of comment from the public. In the second place, the release contained a significant retroactive feature which, in itself, was contrary to appropriate rule making. The firm strongly believed that such an action on the part of the SEC should not go unchallenged by the profession and accordingly sought relief through the injunction process.

On October 5, 1973, the SEC suspended the release and asked for public comments until November 15, 1973. Since this action met the substance of our complaint, the firm thereupon withdrew, without prejudice, its lawsuit against the SEC. On April 11, 1974, the SEC issued Accounting Series Release No. 146A in which the retroactive aspect was eliminated.

PROFESSIONAL PUBLICATIONS

As already indicated, our Committee on Accounting Principles and Auditing Procedures has constituted the basic research body of the firm. Numerous publications have been issued by the Committee which have found wide use in academic and professional circles.

For example, a booklet entitled *Accounting and Reporting Problems of the Accounting Profession* was prepared in 1960, discussing twenty current problem areas in a concise and readable manner. With respect to each topic, the booklet states the problem, the existing practices, our viewpoint, the AICPA position, and the SEC requirements, and it concludes with a brief discussion of our own point of view. The initial purpose was to stimulate discussion and exchange of ideas among our own personnel in furtherance of our "one-voice" concept, but the booklet also proved to be of wide interest in academic circles and has been used extensively in advanced accounting classes. Subsequent editions were issued in 1962, 1969 and 1973, revising and updating the discussions of the twenty subjects and adding six more topics.

Over the years, the committee has prepared comprehensive discussion memorandums presenting our views on subjects under study by the AICPA Director of Accounting Research, Accounting Principles Board and other

AICPA committees. These have been published in booklet form on the following subjects: the postulate of accounting; accounting for income taxes; accounting for the costs of pension plans; accounting for leases; business combinations and intangible assets; accounting changes; and accounting for oil and gas exploration and development costs.

Numerous briefs have been prepared for the Financial Accounting Standards Board and the Securities and Exchange Commission relating to hearings and proposals of these organizations. These briefs and memorandums are the result of extensive study and research by the firm on these subjects.

George R. Catlett, Chairman, and Norman Olson, Vice Chairman of the firm's Committee, were asked by the AICPA to undertake a research study of accounting for goodwill. This study was published by the AICPA in 1968 as *Accounting Research Study No. 10: Accounting for Goodwill.* Although its conclusions were not generally accepted by the profession, it was a sound and well reasoned statement of the position that goodwill should be deducted directly from stockholders' equity. The firm continues to hold this view and it is hoped that eventually it, too, will win wider acceptance.

Early in the 1970's, in recognition of the continuing urgent need for a definition by the accounting profession of the objectives of financial statements, the firm undertook its own study of this problem and in 1972, it produced a volume entitled *Objectives of Financial Statements for Business Enterprises.* The purpose of this book was to set forth what we regarded as the objectives of financial statements and to show how their adoption could result in progress in resolving accounting problems. While it generally reflects the philosophies that have guided the firm over the years in matters of accounting and financial reporting, the book also presents ideas for progress and improvement that in many cases will require some time to achieve. It was written with a view toward stimulating the kind of discussion both within and without the firm that will provide assistance to the profession as a whole in the search for agreement on the objectives of financial statements and in the continuing efforts to improve financial reporting.

The firm is publishing a series of books on *Cases in Public Accounting Practice,* the first volume of which was published in 1960. This series is intended to fill the need that has long existed for a source to which practitioners, professors and students could turn for the record of the principal cases that have established important precedents in the practice of public accounting. These cases are reported on a factual basis, without editorial comment, and are in a form that is suitable for reference, research and educational purposes. Eleven cases have been published through 1973.

Beginning in 1969, the firm has published a series of books containing selected addresses and articles of some of the firm's principal spokesmen. To date, this series has included the following, some of which already have been referred to elsewhere in this volume:

TITLE	AUTHOR
BEHIND THE FIGURES	Arthur Andersen
A SEARCH FOR FAIRNESS IN FINANCIAL REPORTING TO THE PUBLIC (VOLUMES I AND II)	Leonard Spacek
FOOTSTEPS TOWARD PROFESSIONALISM	Joseph S. Glickauf
IN PURSUIT OF PROFESSIONAL GOALS	George R. Catlett and Norman O. Olson
IN THE PUBLIC INTEREST (FOR RELEASE IN 1974)	Harvey Kapnick

The various items described herein are only a few examples of the firm's contribution to the body of professional literature in the field of accounting and are not a comprehensive listing of our publications in that field.

PARTICIPATION IN PROFESSIONAL ORGANIZATIONS

The personnel of Arthur Andersen & Co. have always been interested in the growth and development of the accounting profession. It must be conceded that because of Leonard Spacek's dissatisfaction with the lack of constructive leadership by the American Institute of Certified Public Accountants in establishing accounting principles, he personally spent a minimal amount of time in Institute activities except for those areas where he believed that the profession's deficiencies in serving the public and business could be corrected. But many others have taken a very active part in the AICPA and in other professional accounting organizations around the world. They have served as officers and committee chairmen and as members of many committees.

In 1934, Paul K. Knight served on a nine-man committee, representing the American Institute of Accountants (as the AICPA was then called) and the American Society of Certified Public Accountants. This committee was established at the request of the then new Securities and Exchange Commission for the purpose of making suggestions to the SEC on the form of financial statements and regulations which might be proper under the Securities Exchange Act of 1934, the simplification of financial statements and related schedules prepared under the Securities Act of 1933, and the use of the same form of financial statements for various filing requirements. Some of the recommendations of this committee were adopted by the SEC from time to time.

The firm was represented on the American Institute's Committee on Accounting Procedure (and its predecessor committee) almost constantly during the existence of that committee, as follows:

> 1934-1935 . . . . Paul Grady
>
> 1936-1937 . . . . Paul K. Knight
>
> 1938-1942 . . . . Carman G. Blough
>
> 1942-1953 . . . . Paul K. Knight (Chairman, 1950-1953)
>
> 1953-1959 . . . . Garrett T. Burns

In 1959, the Committee on Accounting Procedure was succeeded by the Accounting Principles Board. Leonard Spacek served as a member of that Board from 1960 to 1965, when he was followed by George R. Catlett. In 1971, Albert J. Bows, Jr. succeeded Mr. Catlett and continued as a member of the committee until its replacement in 1973 by the new Financial Accounting Standards Board. Within the Institute, an Accounting Standards Executive Committee was established, of which Arthur R. Wyatt is a member.

The firm has been represented on the American Institute's Committee on Auditing Procedure for most of the years since that committee was formed in 1939, as follows:

1939-1942	Paul K. Knight
1942-1944	George Wagner
1947-1953	Garrett T. Burns
1953-1958	William D. Sprague
1958-1965	Albert J. Bows, Jr. (Chairman, 1962-1963)
1965-1968	Norman O. Olson
1968-1970	William D. Hall
1970-1974	Harry T. Magill

Various partners have been members of the Council of the American Institute of Certified Public Accountants. In addition to serving on the Council for several years, Richard Claire was a member of the executive committee for the three years ending in 1963, and was a vice president during the 1961-1962 fiscal year. Albert J. Bows, Jr. is a vice president for the 1973-1974 fiscal year.

Beginning in 1957, when he was appointed chairman of its Committee on Cooperation with Security Companies, Walter Oliphant had an almost continuous record of service with the American Institute as a committee member, council member or officer. In 1967, he was elected a vice president and a member of the Board of Directors; in 1971, he was elected President. He thus became the first Arthur Andersen & Co. partner to hold this high office, and he gave of himself unstintingly in leading the Institute through one of its most formative and eventful years. It was during Mr. Oliphant's tenure of office, for example, that the Financial

Accounting Standards Board (previously discussed in this chapter) and the Financial Accounting Foundation came into being.

A sampling of the offices or appointments in professional societies held by representatives of the firm in non-U. S. countries over the last five years offers further tangible evidence of our extensive participation in professional organizations around the world:

Buenos Aires—

> Homero Braessas—Member, Board of Directors of the Technical Institute of Public Accountants (1970 to date)

Bogotá—

> Alfonso Parra—Member, Board of Directors of the National Institute of Public Accountants (1972 to date)

> Miguel Antequera—Member, Board of Directors of the Academy of Public Accountants (1973)

London—

> Ian Hay Davison—Member, Special Development Policy Committee to study and chart the long-range picture of the Institute of Chartered Accountants of England and Wales (1971)

Melbourne—

> J. K. Little—Member, General Council and Executive Committee of the Australian Institute of Chartered Accountants (1969); Chairman, Accountancy Research Foundation (1969-1972)

México City—

> J. Andrés Ruiz—Member, Executive Committee of the Institute of Public Accountants of México (1969)

> Nicolás Urquiza—Member, Board of Directors of the Colegio (1970-1971); Treasurer (1971); President, Mexican Academy of Tax Study (1971)

> Eduardo González—Member, Board of Directors of the Institute (1972 to date)

Oslo—

> Johan Harr—President, Norwegian Institute of Accountants
> (1969-1972) ; President, Board of Auditors for the Five Nordic
> Countries (1970-1971)

We are indeed proud of the contributions that so many of our people
have made to the ongoing progress of the profession, and we have pledged
ourselves to a continuation of this interest and dedication.

CHAPTER THIRTEEN

The Challenge of the Future

With this record behind us, what now of the years ahead? Everyone knows that the past is but a prologue to the future.

In spite of the worldwide political and economic problems to be met, the world appears to be on the threshhold of a new period of major expansion in international trade and commerce. With rising standards of living throughout the world, with the emerging nations playing a larger role in worldwide economic affairs and with a growing demand for food and shelter and energy, the very survival of the world as we know it will depend in part on an acceleration of trade and a massive increase in the capital investment required to support such an expansion. Through the long course of history, mankind has shown a strong instinct for survival, and we must have confidence that over a period of time solutions will be found to today's survival problems, including those relating to food and energy production, population control and the protection of our environment.

Given a reasonably stable world, we believe that our firm is in a particularly strong position to continue to move forward. Our worldwide organization, developed on the basis of our one-firm concept and owned and managed by national partners residing in many countries, can bring a high level of competence to any client in any country—whether a local company or a multinational organization.

Although we now have offices in almost every major financial center in the world, we are witnessing a continuing demand for additional offices as the less developed countries move into the world's economic mainstream. This is a trend that can be expected to accelerate in the years ahead.

Our new organization structure adopted in 1970 has provided the basic framework for a further growth in our size. When we had reached a total figure of 2,000 in 1956, there were those who ventured the guess that we could double again in size—perhaps we could safely reach 5,000. Today, with total worldwide personnel of over 12,000, we still do not know what the practical limits are to the size of the firm. Although large in total number of people, the firm is comprised of many individual office units which, for the most part, are not large, and they are knit together by many strong ties.

We must, of course, never lose sight of why we exist. We live in an increasingly complex society made up of many individual segments—business, labor, consumers, investors and creditors, to name a few. All have their own self-interests, many of which are conflicting; and yet all are interdependent and all are necessary to a society that accepts the responsibility and the consequences of self-government.

As members of our profession, we are a part of that self-governing process. As public accountants we must "call" the transactions within a segment or between segments as we actually find them. We must assume the responsibility of searching out the facts and of stating them without fear or favor to any group or any individual. If we find that the ground rules for stating these facts are inadequate or wrong, then we must also take the lead in searching for corrective action. To provide that service is the true reason for our existence; and it is this overriding purpose that gives both focus and direction to all that we do. This applies with equal force to every area of our practice and in every country where we operate.

In the final analysis, what the firm becomes in the years ahead will depend in large measure upon the quality of the people who will be the body and spirit of Arthur Andersen & Co. in the future. Hopefully, the foundation built during the first sixty years will stand the test of time and further strengthened from year to year, will prove to be a solid base for the efforts of future generations. It is the younger members of our organization today and those women and men invited to join us in the future who will have the responsibility for building the superstructure. In this rapidly changing world, we, today, can only set the compass for our journey into the future on the basis of the firm's basic goals and objectives that thus far have stood the test of time.

This, then, becomes our greatest challenge for the future: to continuously seek out and to train young men and women who have the potential to be tomorrow's leaders—men and women who have the integrity, the wisdom and the dedication to carry the firm to new heights of achievement.

We recognize, of course, that there will be many problems to be faced in the years ahead, both by the firm and by the profession, but there never has been a time in the history of the firm when there were no problems. We pride ourselves on being problem solvers and we have found that in the process of solving them we grow in wisdom and in strength.

So we look forward eagerly to the challenges of the future. With an unequaled group of dedicated men and women, with a long established tradition for integrity and competence in serving our clients, and with an important role to play in the development of an expanded worldwide economic community, we believe that the greatest accomplishments of Arthur Andersen & Co. are still to be achieved.

Biographical Sketches

The character of any organization reflects the quality of its leadership. This is especially true in a professional firm where both leadership and client responsibilities reach deeply into the organization in the day-to-day administration and operation of a professional practice. In reality, in such a partnership it is the combined leadership of all the partners that achieves the end result.

Over the sixty years of its existence, the firm has been fortunate to have partners in leadership positions dedicated to developing the firm's professional service to clients. It is not possible, in these few pages, to identify all those who have played important roles; but there are presented herein a photograph and certain background data for each of our four chief executives, for the partners who have served as members of the firm's advisory group or board of directors and the chairmen of the Committee on Accounting Principles and Auditing Procedures.

It is hoped that this material will provide some further insight into the history of the firm and will serve as an inspiration to all who study the backgrounds of such partners.

ARTHUR ANDERSEN
1885-1947

OUR FOUR CHIEF EXECUTIVES

Arthur Andersen, Founder

(1913-1947)

Arthur Andersen was born May 30, 1885, in Plano, Illinois, a small town about fifty miles west of Chicago. His parents, John William and Mary Aabye Andersen, had emigrated from Norway in 1882. Soon after his birth, the family returned to Norway for a period of three or four years, after which they came back to the United States and established themselves on the west side of Chicago at Ohio and Damen Streets.

Arthur was the fourth of eight children, six boys and two girls. One of his brothers, Walter H. Andersen, eight years his junior, was to be associated with the firm from 1916 to 1932. John William Andersen died in 1901, five years after the death of his wife. The four younger children were then cared for by various relatives. The older ones, all boys, were on their own.

In 1901, Arthur Andersen was working as a mail boy for Fraser & Chalmers Company on the west side of Chicago, where his father had been a foreman in the foundry department. This company later became a part of Allis-Chalmers Manufacturing Company. His normal day-school education ended with the eighth grade but, with financial help from Mr. William J. Chalmers, he managed to get through high school by working

135

during the day and going to school at night. He was graduated from Atheneum High School, Chicago, in 1903.

In 1906, he married Emma Barnes Arnold. By that time, he had advanced in the Allis-Chalmers organization to the position of assistant to the controller. One of his duties was to assist the auditors, and he found that the work involved in public accounting interested him greatly. He had a fairly good salary and "security," but the urge to get into public accounting had taken hold of him, and the year 1907 found him working on the Chicago staff of Price Waterhouse & Co. The decision to make this change cost this recently married young man about one-third of his immediate income.

ASSOCIATION WITH NORTHWESTERN UNIVERSITY

Arthur Andersen passed the C.P.A. examination in 1908, and was the youngest C.P.A. in Illinois at that time. During the same year, he enrolled as an evening student at the newly organized School of Commerce of Northwestern University. The following year he was asked to teach some of the evening accounting classes, with the title of lecturer.

After leaving Price Waterhouse & Co. in 1911, he became controller of Jos. Schlitz Brewing Company in Milwaukee, commuting to Chicago to continue teaching his evening classes at Northwestern.

In the summer of 1912, Seymour Walton, head of the accounting department at Northwestern, resigned to found his own school of accounting. Charles H. Langer, another member of the accounting faculty, also resigned at this time to join Mr. Walton. The lecture notes, problems and other material for their courses were copyrighted in their individual names, and it all went out the door with the departing professors. This left the School of Commerce in a predicament, since their 1912-1913 bulletin announcing several accounting courses had already been issued.

In this situation, the School turned to Arthur Andersen, appointed him Assistant Professor and Head of the Accounting Department, and asked him to reorganize the department and develop the material for the various courses. He later described this as one of the most strenuous years of his life.

In spite of the difficulties, the accounting courses proceeded on schedule, and from the material which was prepared for these courses Arthur

Andersen developed his *Complete Accounting Course,* which was published in 1917 by Ronald Press. Later editions included several chapters on auditing. If not the first, this is certainly one of the earliest complete accounting courses published in this country. In the revision of the 1917 edition, Mr. Andersen was assisted by David Himmelblau and Eric L. Kohler.

In the fall of 1913, the small public accounting practice of The Audit Company of Illinois, a Chicago firm, became available on the death of its owner, Clarence W. Knisely. Arthur Andersen and his partner, Clarence M. DeLany, purchased this practice and opened their office in the Harris Trust Building, Chicago, on December 1, 1913.

In spite of the pressures which developed from his new venture, Mr. Andersen continued his work at Northwestern University, and in 1915 he was made a full professor of accounting.

During all of this time when he had been teaching and starting a public accounting firm, he had, with unusual courage and tenacity of purpose, been pursuing his own formal education at the University of Chicago and at Northwestern University. In 1917, Northwestern granted him the degree of bachelor of business administration. To say the least, it is unusual for a man to become a professor of accounting on the way to earning his bachelor's degree.

Mr. Andersen continued his teaching at Northwestern until 1922, when he found it necessary to resign in order to devote full time to his growing professional practice. At the time of his resignation, Mr. Andersen assigned his future royalties from his *Complete Accounting Course* to Northwestern University. These royalties aggregated more than $100,000 during the following twenty years.

To complete the account of his association with Northwestern, he was elected to the Board of Trustees in 1927, and served as President of the Board from 1930 to 1932. In 1941, the University conferred on him the degree of doctor of laws, a fitting climax to his academic career at Northwestern as student, teacher and trustee.

COLLATERAL ADVANTAGES OF HIS TEACHING

Arthur Andersen's teaching experience, running concurrently with the first nine years of his public accounting firm, had three collateral advantages. Early in the life of the firm, he became convinced that its future depended on his ability to surround himself with able young men. He had inherited a staff of seven older men when the practice of The Audit Company of Illinois was acquired in 1913, and he quickly discovered that this group was not the material on which to build the kind of public accounting firm he had in mind. He wanted young men, preferably just out of college, who were interested not only in accounting, but also in the analysis of business enterprises and the factors that cause them to succeed or fail. In his teaching, he was getting a good look at a large number of prospective public accountants, and some of them who had the qualities he was looking for became members of the Andersen organization.

Again, his classes sometimes brought him into contact with potential clients, especially after 1917, when he taught for several years a special course on the new wartime income and excess-profits taxes. These classes were attended by a large group of business and professional men. This was very helpful in the early growth of the firm.

Finally, his study and research in preparation for teaching his classes resulted in a thorough grounding in accounting theory, which he was able to test out and apply, month by month, in actual situations as they arose in his accounting practice. The practical application of accounting to business interested him from the start. He was never one to operate in a vacuum of pure theory.

In approaching the idea of founding an accounting firm, Arthur Andersen was convinced that the professional accountant of that day took too narrow and technical a view of the scope of his services to the business community. He believed that the audit, though important, was not an end in itself; that the most important service the public accountant could render to his clients began, rather than ended, with the issuing of the certified financial statements; and that if the auditor had looked behind the figures into the actual operating methods and problems of the business he could render a constructive report that would be of real help to management in solving its day-to-day problems. On this type of service he proposed to build his firm. In this he was far ahead of his time, but it was a very important factor in the growth of the firm, from the early days right down to the present.

To preserve his thinking, which constituted the basic foundation of the firm, in 1970 selected articles and addresses were assembled and published in a book titled, *Behind The Figures.*

HIS QUALITIES

Coupled with his courage and high integrity, Arthur Andersen had an indomitable will to succeed—a will that made him a prodigious producer and gave him a tremendous capacity for work. He also had unusual vision and foresight, which enabled him to take advantage of opportunities as they came along, and which guided him in building his organization. In addition, he possessed a keen intellect, native analytical ability, and sound business judgment.

It was this combination of qualities which enabled Mr. Andersen to start a public accounting firm, without financial backing and with few influential friends, with fees of only $45,000 in its first year (1914), and to develop it during the next fifteen years to an organization of seven offices from New York to Los Angeles, with annual fees of more than two million dollars, truly a remarkable accomplishment.

Unquestionably, Arthur Andersen was the dominant factor in the development of the firm during his lifetime. The business world was quick to sense and make use of his capabilities. This is illustrated by the part he played in the Insull situation, described in more detail in Chapter Three.

HIS ACTIVITIES

In addition to his interest in the educational process, Arthur Andersen was actively concerned with civic and philanthropic affairs. Over the years he took part in the work of such organizations as the Chicago Home for the Friendless, the First Methodist Church of Evanston, The Salvation Army, The Cradle Society, The Chicago Sunday Evening Club and the American Red Cross.

He was proud of his Norwegian ancestry and was active in the Norwegian-American Historical Association, serving as president from 1936 to 1942.

On the professional side, Mr. Andersen was, for a time, chairman of the Illinois Board of C.P.A. Examiners and was president of the Illinois

Society of Certified Public Accountants in 1918-1919. He served on various committees of the American Institute of Accountants (as it was then called) and was chairman of its committee on the definition of earned surplus available for dividends. He was active in the United States Chamber of Commerce, serving on the taxation and finance committees. In 1938, Mr. Andersen was offered the presidency of the New York Stock Exchange, which he declined. The fact that he was considered for this position is evidence of his standing in the business community.

Arthur Andersen was the author of the *Complete Accounting Course,* previously described (Ronald Press—1917), and published the following in pamphlet form: *Financial and Industrial Investigations* (1924), *The Major Problem Created by the Machine Age* (1931), *Duties and Responsibilities of the Comptroller* (1934), *The Future of our Economic System* (1934), *Present Day Problems Affecting the Presentation and Interpretation of Financial Statements* (1935), and *A Layman Speaks* (1941).

In addition to the degree of doctor of laws received in 1941 from Northwestern University, similar degrees were conferred on him by Luther College in 1938 and by St. Olaf College and Grinnell College in 1941. In 1939, King Haakon of Norway honored him with the Commander's Cross of the Royal Order of Saint Olav.

In 1953, Arthur Andersen was elected posthumously to the Accounting Hall of Fame, established in 1950 at The Ohio State University, joining such men as George O. May, Robert Montgomery, and Elijah Watts Sells.

Although Mr. Andersen took pride in his business and professional accomplishments, his home and family were his first consideration. His hobbies were golf, fishing, reading, travel, music and art. His greatest happiness was found in the company of his wife and his three children, Ethyl Bernice, Arthur Arnold and Dorothy Emma.

HIS DEATH

After an illness of several months, Arthur Andersen died on January 10, 1947, at the age of sixty-one. His loss was felt very deeply. Shortly thereafter, the following resolution was adopted by his partners:

> *"Resolved that we, the members of this firm, record with profound sorrow the irreparable loss that we have suffered through*

the untimely death, on January 10, 1947, of our great leader and beloved friend, Arthur Andersen.

"No words of ours can adequately portray the value of the services which he rendered to the community at large, to the firm which he founded, and to us, his partners. Arthur Andersen possessed a brilliant and analytical mind, and an extraordinary ability to apply fairness, common sense and realism to the solution of business problems. His tremendous intellectual capacity never caused him to lose, in the smallest degree, those intensely human qualities of kindliness and thoughtfulness that made him so well beloved by everyone with whom he came in contact; but after all is said, it was in Arthur Andersen's character that he was most truly great. Throughout his business career he labored for what was right, and for what was honest and above reproach. Through his unswerving application of the highest principles to the conduct of the affairs of this firm, he has left us, as a priceless heritage, that reputation for independence and integrity that today is universally associated with the name of Arthur Andersen & Co.

"The principles and ideals of Arthur Andersen will always guide us. We, his partners, upon whom now falls the responsibility for shaping the destiny of the firm, do this day pledge ourselves to continue to follow those high principles of human conduct that have made the firm great under his inspired leadership."

A few years before his death, he wrote an editorial for *The Chronicle*, the quarterly publication of the firm. This editorial is quoted in part:

"About forty-five years ago, my own mother told me in Norwegian, 'Think straight—talk straight' (translated freely). No finer heritage could possibly be passed on from one generation to another. It has been as a firm rock to which I could anchor in a storm. Never has it failed me.

"As the temptations came and went, there was an increasing determination that my own children, and now their children, should be taught that virtue and realism are contained in these simple words. This challenge will never fail anyone in a time of trial and temptation."

"Think straight—talk straight" epitomizes the great tradition which Arthur Andersen left to his firm.

LEONARD SPACEK
1907 -

142

OUR FOUR CHIEF EXECUTIVES

Leonard Spacek

Managing Partner (1947-1963)
Chairman (1963-1970)
Senior Partner (1970-1973)

In the tradition of Arthur Andersen, Leonard Spacek went to work at an early age and came up the hard way. He was born September 12, 1907, in Cedar Rapids, Iowa, the second of three sons. His father, Leo Spacek, was a mechanic for Cherry-Burrell Corporation. His mother, Emma Cejka Spacek, became seriously ill and was hospitalized for many years.

Leo Spacek bought a forty-acre farm, and he and his three sons "bached" it there for a period, until his income proved insufficient to maintain the home. From the time Leonard was eight years old until he was thirteen he lived with farm families in the neighborhood. He worked for his board, doing farm chores mornings and evenings, and going to school during the day.

About the time he entered high school his father moved into Cedar Rapids. There, Leonard had a paper route, and farmed out two routes to other boys. He also operated a bicycle shop and did a good business buying up old bicycles for a nominal price, salvaging the good parts and assembling them to sell for five to ten dollars.

Leonard worked for a time as tool boy in a Ford garage, and in 1924, at the age of seventeen, he got a job with Iowa Electric Light and Power Company. His purpose in joining this company was to become an electrical engineer, but because there were no openings in that department, he started in the accounting department. By 1925, he had completed his evening high school courses and started on some evening courses in the liberal arts at Coe College in Cedar Rapids.

During a part of this period, he not only worked during the day in the accounting department, but he also held down an evening job as trouble dispatcher on the switchboard for the entire Iowa Electric Light and Power system. He took the evening job so that he could earn while he was studying. This combination produced a schedule which ran from 7 A.M. until midnight seven days a week. About two years of this grind gave him a very adequate preparation for the rigours of public accounting.

HE JOINS ARTHUR ANDERSEN & CO.

The company for which Leonard Spacek worked was a client of our firm. Since he had worked up to the job of general-ledger accountant, he had numerous contacts with our men, such as Paul Grady, Robert Sellman, Lloyd Witter, and John Jirgal, the partner in charge of public utility work. He had taken the Walton and the International correspondence courses in accounting, and had decided that accounting, not electrical engineering, was to be his field. His work in assisting our men on the annual audit and on special tax matters had interested him, and he decided to apply for a position on our staff. He was accepted, and on Saturday, December 1, 1928, the fifteenth anniversary of the founding of the firm, he reported for work in our Chicago office. He was twenty-one years old at that time.

When he left Cedar Rapids, Leonard Spacek had an understanding with Miss Libbie Smatlan, a co-worker at the Iowa Electric Light and Power Company, that they would be married as soon as he was "established." In 1929, he was getting $125.00 a month and was far from being established, but his marriage took place on January 19 of that year in Kansas City, where he was on a job for the firm. The Spaceks have two children, Bruce Arnold and Judith Ann (Barnes) both of whom are married.

Mr. Spacek was made a manager in 1934, and a partner in 1940. At that time he was placed in charge of the public utility work of the firm, John Jirgal having resigned in 1938. In 1945, he was put in charge of the Chicago office and in 1947, was made managing partner of the firm after the death of Arthur Andersen. He continued in the dual role of managing partner and partner in charge of the Chicago office until 1955, when Donald J. Erickson, who had been in charge of the Cleveland office since its establishment in 1946, took over the responsibility of the Chicago office.

On December 1, 1963, the thirty-fifth anniversary of his joining Arthur Andersen & Co. and the fiftieth anniversary of the firm, Mr. Spacek moved from managing partner to a newly created office of chairman of the partners. In 1970 he became a senior partner when Mr. Harvey Kapnick succeeded him in this position. He continued to play an active role in the firm's affairs until his retirement on July 1, 1973, and during this period he accelerated his efforts to bring about a major improvement in accounting standards in the profession. His addresses and articles form a public record of Mr. Spacek's struggle in this regard and the more important of these has been assembled and published in two volumes titled *A Search for Fairness*.

HIS ACTIVITIES

Over the long span of his professional career, Mr. Spacek gave generously of his time and talents to his community. The organizations that he served in one capacity or another were legion, and a listing of a few of them shows the wide-ranging scope of his concerns. He was a board member or trustee of such organizations as the Chicago Association of Commerce and Industry, Community Fund of Chicago, Lyric Opera of Chicago (life trustee), Goodwill Industries, The John Crerar Library, Museum of Science and Industry (honorary life trustee) and Evanston Hospital Association. At one time or another, he was general chairman of the Metropolitan Crusade for Mercy, president of The Commercial Club and treasurer of the Chicago Alliance of Businessmen.

In the field of education, he was a trustee of Northwestern University, Coe College (life member) and Lake Forest Academy and a member of the citizens' boards of the University of Chicago and the University of Illinois.

On the national scene, he was a trustee from 1965 to 1971 of the International Chamber of Commerce, Inc., a member of the Industry Advisory Council to the Secretary of Defense from 1968 to 1973 and a consultant to the U. S. Bureau of the budget from 1964 to 1973.

In 1962, Mr. Spacek was granted a Doctor of Laws degree by Coe College and in 1967, a Doctor of Humane Letters degree by the National College of Education. In 1973, the Loyola University 1973 Damen award was presented to him for ". . . his dedication to God, society and to the nation"; and on April 22, 1974, the Cost Accounting Standards Board in Washington, D.C. gave him its first public service award. In 1970, he received the Knight's Cross, First Class, of the Royal Order of St. Olav from the King of Norway.

Shortly before his retirement, Mr. Spacek was honored at a dinner attended by two hundred couples representing the business and civic leadership groups of Chicago. After various personal tributes, the group presented a plaque bearing the inscription "Incomparable Accountant, Educator, Management Advisor, Patron of the Arts and Gentleman", and Mayor Richard Daley presented him with the Chicago Medal of Merit.

Although Leonard Spacek's active career with the firm ended with his retirement on July 1, 1973, he left a stamp on the organization that will remain for many years to come.

WALTER OLIPHANT
1917 -

146

OUR FOUR CHIEF EXECUTIVES

Walter Oliphant

Managing Partner (1963-1970)
Senior Partner (1970-1972)

Walter J. Oliphant was born in Oak Park, Illinois on April 16, 1917. His father, Walter C. Oliphant, of Scottish descent, was employed by what later was to become the Railway Express Company as assistant general auditor. His mother, May, of Norwegian descent, was the daughter of Kolben Johnson, a Chicago manufacturer who had a number of mechanical inventions to his credit.

His boyhood life was spent in Oak Park, Illinois, where he attended the Oak Park and River Forest Township High School. During his high school years he played varsity basketball and tennis, and was manager of the football team. While in high school, Wally also worked for a time as a special delivery mail boy for the Kenilworth, Illinois post office, and later as a ticket agent for the North Shore Suburban Railroad, which has long since gone out of business. He was also involved in a number of school activities and particularly interested in Hi-Y, of which he was president. It was through this activity that he became acquainted with Lawrence Aplin, who later was to have a considerable influence on his life.

COLLEGE DAYS

At Dr. Aplin's urging, Wally attended Northwestern University where he graduated in 1939 with a degree of Bachelor of Science in Commerce. While in college, he was elected vice-president of the student alumni association and was involved in several other campus organizations. He was active in intramural athletics and was selected as a member of several all-star teams.

In order to help finance his college education, Wally maintained a heavy work schedule. He worked as a floor manager of the Evanston store of Marshall Field & Co., while at the same time serving as a University janitor for two hours a night, after which, for a brief period, he worked at the soda fountain of the campus grill for three hours each night. He also worked as a waiter in one of the sorority houses for his meals during all four years.

Wally was rushing chairman for his fraternity, and takes pride in the fact that his first pledgee was Robert I. Jones, who later became his roommate while in school. He was also president of his fraternity, a local fraternity which applied for and obtained national association with Alpha Delta Phi during his term. During his senior year and for two years afterward Wally played industrial league basketball and baseball in the Chicago area.

It was while Wally was in his senior year at Northwestern that he met the attractive and vivacious young nurse who was to become Mrs. Oliphant. Wally was one of those who succumbed to the flu in 1938, and when confined in the university hospital, it was Marjorie who nursed him back to health. The Oliphants have four children—Lee, Jill and Diane, all happily married, and a son, Gary, who has just completed his academic work at Yale, where he has been for all three years of competition one of Yale's star performers on the swimming team.

TIME OUT FOR THE NAVY

Wally joined the Chicago office of the firm immediately after graduation on July 5, 1939. With the advent of World War II, he entered service with the U. S. Navy. He served most of his Navy career with the Bureau of Supplies and Accounts, where he was involved with John Higgins and Joseph Glickauf in the development of many of the procedures adopted by the Navy in the financial area during the war. They served together as three of a four-man team in industrial management. John and Wally had worked together before the war in the Chicago office. It was their combined efforts that persuaded Mr. Glickauf to join the firm after the war, and all three of these men continued to work closely together for many years.

HE MOVES INTO ADMINISTRATION

Mr. Oliphant was named administrative assistant to Mr. Spacek in 1950 while a manager in the Chicago office. Two years later he was admitted to the firm, and in April 1953 he transferred to the Boston office as partner in charge. He remained in Boston for six years, during which time the office achieved its first significant growth, with personnel rising from 26 to 96 people in that period.

Upon his return to Chicago in 1959, he assumed the position of director of operations for the United States and Canada, which role he filled until his assumption of the managing partner's position on December 1, 1963, the 50th anniversary of the founding of the firm. He continued as managing partner until 1970, when he asked to be relieved of his responsibilities as the firm's chief executive office. He was immediately elected to a newly created position of vice chairman of the partners and soon thereafter as a senior partner.

In 1971, Mr. Oliphant was elected president of the American Institute of Certified Public Accountants where he served the profession with great distinction during one of the more formative years of the Institute's history. While in that capacity, he and Mrs. Oliphant travelled extensively throughout the United States and to various parts of the world, representing the United States profession and handling a heavy schedule of speaking engagements.

HIS ACTIVITIES

In addition to his active participation in the affairs of the American Institute of Certified Public Accountants and the Illinois Society of Certified Public Accountants over a long period of years, including membership on the Institute's board of directors from 1967 to 1973 and its council from 1966 for life, Mr. Oliphant was deeply involved in both civic and academic affairs.

He was a member of the boards of such organizations as the United Charities of Chicago, The Community Fund of Chicago, the Chicago Area Council of the Boy Scouts of America (vice president), and the Young Men's Christian Association. He has been a member of the Chicago Crime Commisison since 1964 (director, 1967-1970) and a member of the Illinois Council on Economic Education. Over the years, he served as chairman of a number of annual fund drives including United Charities, United Settlement Appeal and the Chicago Council of Boy Scouts of America.

In the academic field, Mr. Oliphant was a member of the Board of Overseers of The Amos Tuck School of Business Administration at Dartmouth College from 1965 to 1972, an Alumni Regent of Northwestern University (alumni vice president 1964 to 1967 and treasurer 1963), chairman of the board of John Evans Club at Northwestern University since 1966 and a life member, and a member of advisory boards or councils at Tulane University, University of Chicago, Northwestern University, University of Illinois and National College of Education. In 1966, he received the Award of Merit from Northwestern University and its Service Award in 1969.

By the end of 1972 Mr. Oliphant chose to retire from the firm. Because of his interest in young people, especially at the college level, he had for many years nurtured the thought of teaching at a business school. This plan has been realized by his having been offered a professorship at the Amos Tuck School of Business Administration at Dartmouth College, Hanover, New Hampshire. As he teaches for only one quarter each year, it leaves time for him to participate in a number of community and professional activities in addition to enjoying a more relaxed pace of living.

HARVEY KAPNICK
1925 -

OUR FOUR CHIEF EXECUTIVES

Harvey Kapnick

Chairman, 1970-

Harvey Edward Kapnick, Jr. was born June 16, 1925 in Palmyra, Michigan. His father, Harvey, was a farmer whose father had emigrated from Germany. His mother, Beatrice Bancroft, had been raised in Toledo, Ohio, although her parents had lived near Palmyra in their youth and returned to this area while Harvey was in school. The farms on which he was raised with a brother and sister still remain in the family.

During his years at Adrian High School he worked in a grocery store. But despite the time he devoted to helping his father on the farm and to the grocery store job, he still found time to actively participate in school activities. His interest in the Forensic League (of which he was president) and in the debating team helped him develop a trait that would be useful in later years—the desire and ability to speak out for his beliefs. He also served as Junior Class president, president of his 4-H Club, and associate editor of his high school annual. He received the University of Michigan Honor Trophy at his high school for "outstanding achievement in scholarship, athletics and leadership."

COLLEGE AND MILITARY YEARS

High school graduation in 1942 found Harvey with very little money but wanting a college education. He enrolled at Cleary College in Ypsilanti,

Michigan, only 35 miles from his home, and to provide funds to pay for his college expenses, over and above those provided by his parents and other relatives, he borrowed money from a scholarship fund and again worked in a grocery store and at a funeral home. His college major, accounting, was the result of an interesting high school accounting course as well as his feeling that a career in public accounting would provide him with an opportunity to be an independent entrepreneur.

In 1943 the United States was involved in World War II and Harvey, after reaching eighteen, decided to interrupt his college career and volunteer for military service. He joined the Army Air Force in July 1943, and after a short period at James Milliken University in Decatur, Illinois, and other basic training, he was on his way to the Southwest Pacific where he participated in campaigns in New Guinea and Leyte, one of the islands in the Philippines. Although it was unusual for a man serving in a combat area to be chosen for Officer Candidate School, Harvey was selected to attend the Officer Candidate School at Brisbane, Australia, and was promoted to Second Lieutenant on June 1, 1945. He went on to serve on the Air Evaluation Board and to assist in researching the effectiveness of the Army Air Force in Southwest Pacific areas. He was given the Army commendation award "for outstanding service in the line of duty," as well as the American Theater Medal, the Victory Medal, the Philippine Liberation Ribbon, and six bronze stars for having participated in six specific areas of the Asiatic Pacific Theater.

After his Army discharge in 1946, Harvey went back to Cleary College and after receiving his Bachelor of Science degree in April, 1947, went to the University of Michigan to enroll in graduate study. Because Michigan would not accept his Bachelor's degree for course work toward a Master's degree, he was admitted as a special student. He took the same courses, but was not able to apply them toward an advanced degree. In 1971 he received the honorary degree of Doctor of Science in Business Administration from Cleary College.

HE JOINS ARTHUR ANDERSEN & CO.

Mr. Kapnick joined the Chicago office of Arthur Andersen & Co. in 1948, after his year of study at the University of Michigan. He had had Herbert Miller and William Paton as professors, and both urged him to investigate opportunities at the firm. He did, and found that Arthur Andersen & Co. offered him just what he was looking for — a chance to do well on his own merits and hard work, and thus an opportunity to become an entrepreneur in what he considered to be the finest public accounting firm in the country.

Eight years later, in 1956, Mr. Kapnick became a partner in the firm, and shortly thereafter he was placed in charge of the merchandising industry division of the Chicago office. In 1962, he moved to the Cleveland office as managing partner where he stayed until 1970. In 1966, he was made a member of the firm's advisory committee and its successor the new board of directors in 1968.

In May, 1970, when Walter Oliphant moved from managing partner of the firm to a senior partner, Mr. Kapnick returned to Chicago upon his election as the firm's fourth chief executive. Shortly thereafter, Leonard Spacek also became a senior partner, and at that time Harvey was elected chairman of the firm. He has spoken widely on many important issues in the accounting profession, and has published many of such speeches in the book *In the Public Interest*.

HIS FAMILY

During his college years, he met and married his first wife, Jean Bradshaw. She had also attended Cleary College and was from Cass City, Michigan. She passed away shortly after their move to Cleveland in 1962. Later he married Mary Redus Johnson, the widow of L. Byron Johnson, a former manager in the firm and immediately preceding his death in 1962 a senior officer of the Hertz Corporation. The Kapnicks have three sons, David, a student at Duke University in North Carolina; Brad, a student at Stanford University in California; and Scott, a student at New Trier West High School in Winnetka, Illinois.

HIS ACTIVITIES

Mr. Kapnick has not only had time for his family and his professional career, but has also been very active in civic and community affairs. Since his early years as a staffmember, he has given great amounts of time and effort to the communities in which he has lived. In Cleveland he was actively involved in the American Cancer Society, the Society for Crippled Children, the Boy Scouts of America, the Bluecoats, the Cleveland Citizens' League, the Blossom Music Center, the Lake Erie Opera Theatre, the Northern Ohio Children's Performing Music Foundation, Inc., the Cleveland Plan, the Christ Church Foundation, and he was president of the Shaker Heights Country Club.

In Chicago his activities have included the Chicago Home for the Friendless, the American Cancer Society, the Chicago Symphony Orchestra, the Ravinia Festival Association, the Metropolitan Crusade of Mercy, the YMCA Advisory Board, the Chicago 21 Corporation (a private organization to develop an entirely new south loop city), the Museum of Science and Industry, the American Red Cross, and the Sunday Evening Club. He was also cochairman of the task force to review and improve the control over welfare spending established by Governor Daniel Walker in 1972.

On a national level he has been involved in the Menninger Foundation, the International Executive Service Corps, the National Legacies Committee of the United Nations and the Chamber of Commerce of the United States.

In the field of education he is a member of the Board of Trustees for Siena Heights College in Adrian, Michigan, a member of the Advisory Council of the Graduate School of Business of Northwestern University, a member of the Board of Visitors for Duke University Graduate School of Business Administration, and a member of the Council on the Graduate School of Business of the University of Chicago.

Professionally, Mr. Kapnick has been a member of the American Institute of Certified Public Accountants and the Ohio and Illinois Society of Certified Public Accountants. He has served as a member of the AICPA council and on several professional committees of these groups. He is also a member of the American Accounting Association and the National Association of Accountants.

MEMBERS OF THE ADVISORY GROUP
AND THE BOARD OF DIRECTORS;
AND THE CHAIRMEN OF THE COMMITTEE
ON ACCOUNTING PRINCIPLES
AND AUDITING PROCEDURES

GUY BARBIER
Advisory Group—1967-1968
Board of Directors—1969-

Mr. Barbier was born in Paris in 1928 and was graduated from the Ecole des Hautes Etudes Commerciales, Paris. He joined the Paris office in December, 1954, and worked on the audit staff for three years before transferring to the administrative services division. He spent two years in the New York and Chicago offices and was made a manager on January 1, 1961. In 1964, he became a principal of the firm. He was in charge of the administrative services division in Paris until July, 1967, and is now Managing Partner of the Paris office as well as Country Managing Partner—France.

WILLIAM P. BARSANTI
Advisory Group—1966-1968

Mr. Barsanti came from Tonopah, Nevada, and was born in 1923 of Italian ancestry. He was graduated from the University of California with honors in 1948 and also received his Master's degree. Starting with the San Francisco office in 1949, Mr. Barsanti transferred to the Paris office as a manager in 1955, became regional supervisor for the Brussels, Milan, and Oslo offices in 1957, and in 1959 moved to Milan as regional supervisor for Southern Europe; he was admitted to partnership in 1960. In 1967, he transferred to New York and then to Rome as Managing Partner in 1970.

JOE D. BEASLEY
(Deceased—June 4, 1966)
Advisory Group—1955-1957
(Vice Chairman—1956-1957)

Mr. Beasley was born in Alamogordo, New Mexico, on April 4, 1902. He received a Bachelor of Arts degree from the University of Texas in 1922 and attended the graduate school of Columbia University. He joined the firm in our New York office on October 27, 1924. He became a manager in 1929 and on October 1, 1937 was the initial manager in charge of the newly opened Houston office. He was admitted to partnership in 1940 and continued as Managing Partner of the Houston office until May 4, 1961, at which time he became an advisory partner.

F. MERRILL BEATTY
Advisory Group—1947-1956

Mr. Beatty was born in Chicago and was graduated from the University of Illinois. He was employed by the Chicago office in 1923, became a manager in 1929, and a partner in 1937, at which time he was transferred to the New York office. He specialized in regulated industries work during this entire period and was head of the division from 1947 through 1963. He became a partially retired partner on July 1, 1966, and fully retired July 1, 1972.

ALBERT J. BOWS, JR.
Advisory Group—1957-1960;
1963-1966
(Vice Chairman—1958-1959
Chairman—1959-1960)
Board of Directors—1968-

Mr. Bows was born in Chicago in 1913 and raised in Wilmette, Illinois. He joined the Chicago office on graduation from Northwestern University in 1935 and was transferred to Atlanta in 1941. He became a manager in 1943, a partner in 1950, and was Managing Partner of the Atlanta office from 1959 to 1969. He became a Senior Partner in 1971.

RICHARD C. BRANDT
(Deceased—August 23, 1957)
Chairman, Committee on
Accounting Principles and
Auditing Procedures—1957-1958

Mr. Brandt was born in Detroit, Michigan in 1912. He was employed by the firm in Chicago on July 1, 1936, shortly after he received his Master's degree from the Univerisity of Michigan. Mr. Brandt was transferred to the Detroit office in 1940 and became a manager in 1943. He left the firm temporarily, rejoining in 1948. He became a partner in 1951. Mr. Brandt was elected Vice Chairman of the Committee on Accounting Principles and Auditing Procedures in 1954 and Chairman in May, 1957.

JAMES J. BRICE
Board of Directors—1968-

Mr. Brice, who was born in 1925, was graduated from Northwestern University in 1950. He spent one year with Standard Oil Co. of Indiana and started with the Chicago office of the firm in 1951. He became a manager in 1956, a partner in 1960, and in September, 1968, transferred to the Los Angeles office to become Managing Partner. In 1972 he transferred to Chicago and became Vice Chairman—Chicago.

RENICK H. BUCKLES
Advisory Group—1947-1948; 1958-1959

Mr. Buckles came from Champaign, Illinois. He attended theUniversity of Illinois and graduated in June, 1932. He was employed by the firm in October, 1932. The firm had relatively few offices then, and Mr. Buckles spent the first nine years traveling throughout the United States on various regulated industries audit and systems assignments. He became a manager January 1, 1941, was admitted to the firm on January 1, 1945, and was Managing Partner of the San Francisco office from November 1, 1945, to November 1, 1965. He retired on June 30, 1972.

WILLIAM CAMM
Advisory Group—1964-1967

Mr. Camm was born and raised in Los Angeles. He received his B.S. degree from the University of Southern California in 1946. After service as a supply officer in the United States Navy, Mr. Camm was employed by the Los Angeles office in 1948. He became a manager in 1953 and a partner in 1957. Later that year he moved to Cincinnati as Managing Partner of that office, a position he occupied until June 1, 1972, when he became Managing Partner of the Los Angeles office.

JAMES A. CAMPBELL
Advisory Group—1959-1962
(Vice Chairman—1960-1961
Chairman—1961-1962)
Board of Directors—1968-1969

Mr. Campbell was born in Brooklyn, New York, in 1911. He came with the firm June 4, 1934 and has worked in our New York, Chicago, and Los Angeles offices. He became a manager in 1941 and a partner in 1948. He has served in our regulated industries, commercial, tax and administrative services departments. He was Managing Partner of the Los Angeles office from 1951 to July 1, 1966. He became a Senior Partner in 1973. Mr. Campbell is a graduate of Harvard University, where he also obtained his Master's degree.

LEE S. CARTER

Advisory Group—1961-1962;
1966-1968

Mr. Carter was born in 1923 and grew up in Denver, Colorado. He attended Villanova College and the Harvard Business School (M.B.A., 1947). He came with the firm (Kansas City office) on January 20, 1950. After two years on the audit staff, he transferred to the administrative services division. He became a manager in 1955 and a principal in 1960. He was in charge of the administrative services division in Kansas City from 1956 until 1971. In 1972 he transferred to the Mexico City office as Director of Administrative Services Practice for México, Puerto Rico and South America, and in 1973 relocated to the San Juan office.

GEORGE R. CATLETT

Chairman, Committee on
Accounting Principles and
Auditing Procedures—1962-

Mr. Catlett was born in 1917 and grew up in Fairmount, Illinois. He obtained his B.S. and M.S. degrees from the University of Illinois. He was employed by the Chicago office in 1940 and left in 1942 for four years as an officer in procurement work for the Army Ordnance Corps. He became a manager in 1946 and a partner in 1952, and was engaged primarily in commercial auditing. He transferred to St. Louis in 1953. In 1958 he returned to Chicago and in 1962 became Chairman of the Committee on Accounting Principles and Auditing Procedures.

WILBUR S. DUNCAN_____
Advisory Group—1963-1966
(Vice Chairman—1964-1965
Chairman—1965-1966)

Mr. Duncan was born in 1919 and was raised in Texas. He graduated from Columbia University in New York. He was employed by the New York office in 1947, became a manager in 1952, and a partner in 1956. He is a Director—Accounting and Auditing Practice, operating out of the New York and Stamford offices.

STEPHEN ELLIOTT_____
Advisory Group—1967-1968

Mr. Elliott was born in London, England, in 1920 and received his formal education there. He is a Fellow of the Institute of Chartered Accountants of Ontario and also of the Institute of Chartered Accountants in England and Wales. He joined another public accounting firm in Toronto in 1947 and was admitted as a partner of that firm in 1955. He became Managing Partner of the Toronto office in 1960 and is also Country Managing Partner—Canada.

DONALD ERICKSON
Advisory Group—1955-1959;
1965-1967
Board of Directors—1968-
(Chairman—1968-   )

Mr. Erickson was born in Madison, Wisconsin. He was employed by the Chicago office in 1936 after graduation from the University of Wisconsin. In 1941 he transferred to the Detroit office as a member of the regulated industries division, and in 1946 he transferred to Cleveland where he had the responsibility to open and to be in charge of that office. In 1947 he was admitted to the partnership, and in 1955 he returned to Chicago to become Managing Partner of the Chicago office. He has been chairman of the board of directors since its organization in 1968.

E. A. EVENSON
Advisory Group—1956-1959

Mr. Evenson was born in 1918 in North Dakota and was graduated from the University of North Dakota. He was employed by the Chicago office in 1937 and transferred to the Los Angeles office in 1940. He served in the United States Navy from 1943 until 1946, became a manager on July 1, 1946, and was admitted to the firm on July 1, 1952. He was Managing Partner of the Los Angeles office from July 1, 1966, to September 1, 1968. He is a Director—Accounting and Auditing Practice.

DONALD M. GAMET

Advisory Group—1958-1961
(Vice Chairman—1959-1960
Chairman—1960-1961)
Board of Directors—1968-

Mr. Gamet was born in 1916. He obtained his B.S. degree from Ft. Hays Kansas State College and M.B.A. and LL.B degrees from the University of Kansas. He then taught accounting and economics at Friends University, Wichita, Kansas. He came with the Kansas City office in 1942, became a manager in 1946, a partner in 1954, and was Managing Partner of the Kansas City office from 1956 to September, 1970, when he transferred to Chicago to become Vice Chairman—Tax Practice.

MARVIN K. HAMBRICK

Advisory Group—1961-1964

Mr. Hambrick, born in 1921, is from Oklahoma City and is a graduate of the University of Oklahoma. He was employed by the Houston office on August 1, 1949, became a manager in the tax department in 1952, and was admitted to the firm on July 1, 1958. In 1957 he transferred to the Oklahoma City office and was in charge of that office from 1958 until May 31, 1973, when he left the firm to become Vice President—Finance of Kerr-McGee Corporation.

JOHN L. HENNESSY
Advisory Group—1960-1963
(Vice Chairman—1961-1962
Chairman—1962-1963)
Board of Directors—1968-

Mr. Hennessy was born in 1917 and came from Boston, Massachusetts. He graduated from Boston College in Chestnut Hill, Massachusetts, with his A.B. degree, and the Harvard School of Business with his M.B.A. He was employed by our New York office in 1946 after serving two years in the United States Navy. He was promoted to manager in 1951 and became a partner in 1957. He became Managing Partner of the Hartford office when it was opened in 1961. In 1963, he transferred to Chicago as the Managing Partner—United States and Canada. In 1972, he became a Senior Partner.

DANIEL R. HICKEN
Advisory Group—1965-1968

Mr. Hicken was born in Heber City, Utah, on December 31, 1919. He attended Brigham Young University and the University of Utah, receiving his B.S. degree from the latter school in 1945. Upon graduation, he accepted employment in our Los Angeles office where he has remained since that date. On July 1, 1951, he was promoted to manager, and in 1957 he was admitted to the partnership. Since 1957 he has had partner responsibility for the firm's world-wide Small Business Competency Program.

JOHN A. HIGGINS
(Deceased—October 27, 1965)
Advisory Group—1956-1965
(Chairman—1958-1959)

Mr. Higgins, born in North Dakota in 1913, attended St. Thomas College and was graduated from the University of Minnesota in 1938. After three years in the Chicago office, he left for a brief interlude with IBM. He was in the Navy from 1942 to 1945 and was reemployed as a senior in Chicago in January, 1946. He became a manager on July 1, 1946, and a year later went to Los Angeles as head of administrative services. He returned to our Chicago office in 1950, was admitted to the firm on July 1, 1951, and placed in charge of the administrative services division of the entire firm. Mr. Higgins was elected to the newly-created position of Director of Administration on July 1, 1957, and continued in that capacity until his death.

GALE HITCHCOCK
Advisory Group—1963-1966

Mr. Hitchcock was born in Ohio in 1922 and received a B.S. degree from Ohio University in 1946 following three years in the United States Army Signal Corps. Upon graduation he joined the staff of our Detroit office, where he became a manager in 1951 and a principal of the firm in 1956. He is in charge of administrative services in the Detroit office and a Practice Director—Administrative Services.

MARVIN JOHNSON
Advisory Group—1959-1962

Mr. Johnson was born January 12, 1919 and was graduated with a B.S. degree from the University of Illinois in 1940. He joined the staff of our New York office August 1, 1940 and after serving three years as an officer in the United States Navy reported back to work in January, 1946. He became a manager in July, 1946, and transferred to our Philadelphia office in October, 1946. He transferred back to the New York office in September, 1948. He became a partner July 1, 1952 and in July, 1953, transferred to Chicago as Partner in Charge of Coordination of Office Management. In January, 1955, he transferred to Cleveland as Managing Partner. He resigned March 31, 1962.

CHARLES W. JONES
(Deceased—June 30, 1970)
Advisory Group—1947-1956
(Vice Chairman—1947-1955)
Chairman of Committee on
Accounting Principles and
Auditing Procedures—1946-1957

Mr. Jones was born in 1889 and raised in Illinois. He was graduated from the University of Wisconsin in 1914, when he joined the staff of our Chicago office. He was promoted to manager in 1919, and admitted to partnership in 1924. In 1925, he became partner in charge of the New York office. From 1932 through 1944 he was partner in charge of the Chicago office. From 1947 to 1956 he served as Vice Chairman of the firm. In 1945 he was made chairman of the firm's Committee on Accounting Principles and Auditing Procedures and served in that capacity until 1958. He retired in 1959.

ROBERT I. JONES
Advisory Group—1958-1961
Board of Directors—1968-

Mr. Jones was born in 1920 and was graduated from Northwestern University in 1941 with a B.S. degree in Commerce. He came with the firm immediately following his graduation, becoming a manager in 1947, and was admitted to the firm as a partner in 1952. Mr. Jones has been associated with the firm's Chicago office throughout his entire career. As a partner he was in charge of the Chicago merchandising division as well as the firm's industry program for merchandising until 1957. At that time he assumed responsibility (until 1970) for the firm's overall industry competence program. In 1970 he became Vice Chairman—International Operations.

B. P. KIRKPATRICK
Advisory Group—1962-1965

Mr. Kirkpatrick was born and raised in Los Angeles. After graduation from U.C.L.A. in 1943, he spent three years' active duty with the United States Navy and a number of years with another national firm of accountants. He joined the audit staff of the Los Angeles office in 1952 as a senior, was promoted to manager in 1955, and was admitted to the partnership in 1958.

PAUL K. KNIGHT

(Deceased—August 24, 1957)
Advisory Group—1947-1956
(Chairman—1947-1955)

Mr. Knight was born in Wabash, Indiana on February 9, 1893. He received a Master's Degree from the University of Illinois in 1916 and joined our organization October 8, 1917. He became a manager in 1921 and a partner in 1925. He was in charge of the Kansas City office from 1923 until his transfer to New York in 1925. He was Managing Partner of the New York office from 1932 to 1950 when he became an advisory partner. In 1947 he was elected Chairman of the partnership and served in that capacity for nine years.

F. C. LAWRENCE

(Deceased—September 11, 1969)
Advisory Group—1959-1962

Mr. Lawrence was born in Houston, Texas, in 1916. He was graduated from Rice University with a B.A. degree in 1942 and joined the Houston office in September, 1945. He was promoted to manager in the administrative services division July 1, 1949, and was admitted to the partnership July 1, 1954. He transferred from Houston to Chicago on July 1, 1964, and was named Managing Partner of the Denver office on October 1, 1965.

M. PAUL LeBLANC, JR.⎯⎯⎯⎯⎯
Advisory Group—1960-1963
Board of Directors—1968-

Mr. LeBlanc was born in Baton Rouge, Louisiana, in 1921 and was graduated from Louisiana State University. He was employed by the Houston office in 1949, became a manager in 1953, and a partner in in 1956. From July, 1958, to June, 1966, he was Managing Partner of the New Orleans office. In July, 1966, he transferred to the New York office as Managing Partner of that office. In 1972 he became Vice Chairman—New York area.

MARK D. LITTLER⎯⎯⎯⎯⎯
Advisory Group—1955-1957;
1966-1967

Mr. Littler was born in Illinois in 1911 and was graduated from the University of Illinois in 1933. He was employed by the Chicago office in 1933 and was transferred to the Milwaukee office in 1938. He became a manager in 1940 and a partner in 1945, at which time he went to London, where he was in charge of our work in Europe for a period of three years. Upon returning from London in 1948, he was assigned to the New York office. He transferred to the Detroit office in 1952 and was Managing Partner of that office until December, 1969. He was named a Senior Partner in 1972.

EDWARD E. MALTBY

Advisory Group—1964-1967
(Vice Chairman—1965-1966
Chairman—1966-1967)

Mr. Maltby was born in London, in 1911. He was articled with an accounting firm in London and shortly after qualifying became a partner. In 1946 he joined the London office of a New York law firm as consultant on United Kingdom and United States tax. In 1959 he joined our London office as head of the tax department, was admitted to the firm in 1961, and was Managing Partner of the London office from October 1, 1963 to July 1, 1966. He was then Director of Operations for Europe and Africa until 1970, and served as Country Managing Partner—United Kingdom, Ireland, and South Africa until 1973, when he became a Senior Partner.

JOHN W. MARCH

Advisory Group—1962-1965
(Vice Chairman—1963-1964
Chairman—1964-1965)
Board of Directors—1973-

Mr. March was born in Cleveland, Ohio, in 1923. He graduated from the University of Wisconsin and joined the staff of the Milwaukee office in 1945. He transferred to the Chicago office in 1950, and was promoted to manager and transferred to the Boston office in 1951. He became a partner in 1956 and was Managing Partner of the Boston office from 1959 until September 1, 1965, at which date he assumed duties in the Chicago office in connection with the firm-wide functional responsibility of our commercial and industrial client practice. He presently is Vice Chairman—Accounting and Auditing Practice.

ROBERT L. MAY_____
Advisory Group—1966-1968
Board of Directors—1970-

Mr. May was born in 1923, and was raised in Dupo, Illinois. Upon graduation from the University of Illinois in 1948, he was employed by the New York office. He became a manager in 1953, and a partner in 1957. Over the years he has been responsible for handling some of our largest international clients.

RANDAL B. McDONALD_____
Board of Directors—1969-1972

Mr. McDonald, who was born in 1930, was raised in El Campo, Texas. He graduated from Wharton Junior College and joined the Houston office in June, 1952, after graduation from the Univerisity of Texas. He became a manager on July 1, 1957, in the commercial division and a partner July 1, 1961. He is currently Managing Partner—Natural Resources and a Country Managing Partner—United States.

KEITH B. McKY
Advisory Group—1961-1964
(Vice Chairman—1962-1963
Chairman—1963-1964)

Mr. McKy was born in Blue River, Wisconsin, in 1909. He was graduated from the University of Wisconsin with a Master's degree and was employed by the Wisconsin Public Service Commission in the fall of 1932, where he was engaged in rate case work. He joined the firm in the New York office in September, 1936, was made manager in 1941, and a partner in 1945. He was transferred to the Chicago office where he worked on regulated industries, industrial and manufacturing engagements. As of June 30, 1965, he elected partial retirement and became fully retired on October 31, 1971.

FRED L. MOORE, JR.
Advisory Group—1960-1963
Board of Directors—1972-

Mr. Moore was born in Aurora, Illinois, in 1923. He was graduated from the University of Illinois after three years of military service in World War II. He became a manager in 1952 in the Chicago office, was transferred to Minneapolis in 1954, admitted to partnership in 1957, and became Managing Partner of the Minneapolis office in 1961. He remained in Minneapolis until 1970, when he was transferred to the San Francisco office to become Managing Partner there. He has been a Country Managing Partner—United States since 1972.

THOMAS M. MOORE
Advisory Group—1967-1968

Mr. Moore is a native of North Carolina and was born in 1921. He graduated from the University of North Carolina in 1947 after three years in the United States Navy. He was employed by the Atlanta office in 1947, became a manager in 1952, and was admitted as a partner in 1957. He moved to the Charlotte office as Managing Partner of that office when it was opened.

RUSSELL H. MORRISON
Chairman of Committee on
Accounting Principles and
Auditing Procedures—1958-1962

Mr. Morrison was born in Roberts, Illinois. He graduated from the University of Illinois in 1920. Except for 2½ years (1927-1929) with a public utility group, his business career has been in public accounting practice in Chicago. He came to our firm in 1935, and became a partner in 1941. From July 1957 to April 1971, when he became fully retired, he devoted full time to the firm's Committee on Accounting Principles and Auditing Procedures of which he was chairman from 1958 to 1962.

WILLIAM J. MUELLER
Board of Directors—1972-

Mr. Mueller started with the firm in July, 1941, as an office boy. He attended Northwestern University and Wright Jr. College. He left in 1945 to become comptroller of Dancer-Fitzgerald-Sample, Inc., an advertising agency. In July, 1950, he returned to Arthur Andersen & Co., became a manager in 1952, and a partner in 1956, specializing in merchandising, hospitals, and advertising agencies. He is Vice Chairman —Administrative Services.

HUGH E. NICHOLS
Advisory Group—1947-1956

Mr. Nichols was born in Marshall county, Iowa. He was employed by the firm on September 16, 1924, after graduation from Grinnell College. He became a manager on July 1, 1934, and was admitted to partnership on July 1, 1940. From 1941 until his retirement in 1967 he had firm-wide responsibility for our commercial audit practice.

NORMAN OLSON

*Vice Chairman, Committee on
Accounting Principles and
Auditing Procedures—1964-*

Mr. Olson grew up near St. James, Minnesota, and graduated from St. Olaf College, Northfield, Minnesota. After spending three years in the Navy during World War II, he received his M.A. degree from the University of Minnesota. He was employed by the Chicago office shortly after his graduation in 1948. Mr. Olson was made a manager and transferred to the St. Louis office in 1953, and became a partner in 1958. In 1962, he returned to Chicago as a member of the Committee on Accounting Principles and Auditing Procedures and became Vice Chairman of that committee in 1964.

EARL W. PIERSON

*Advisory Group—1956-1961;
1962-1965
(Chairman—1957-1958)
Board of Directors—1968-1969*

Mr. Pierson was born in Elgin, Illinois, in 1910. He came with the Chicago office in 1933 upon receiving his B.A. degree from the University of Wisconsin. He transferred to Houston in October, 1937, when that office was opened, became a manager in 1942 and a partner in 1949. He was in charge of the Houston office regulated industries division from 1942 to 1961 and was Managing Partner of the Houston office from 1961 to 1968.

J. ANDRÉS RUIZ_____
Board of Directors—1971-

Sr. Ruiz was born in Coatzacoalcos, Vera-cruz, in 1923. After attending high school in the United States, he returned to Méxi-co City where he was graduated from the University of México. Following a year's experience with another accounting firm, he was employed by our México City office on December 7, 1948. He be-came a manager in 1955 and was ad-mitted to the firm in 1960. In 1962, he became Managing Partner of the México City office. He is also Country Managing Partner—México and Central America.

THOMAS A. SAMPSON_____
Board of Directors—1973-

Mr. Sampson is a native of Boston having been born there in 1926. He was grad-uated from Boston College after two years of service in the United States Marine Corps, and he joined the Boston office in June, 1951. He became a manager in 1957 and a partner in 1962. He has been Man-aging Partner of the Boston office since 1965.

ROBERT A. SANDERSON——————————
Advisory Group—1965-1968
(Vice Chairman—1966-1967
Chairman—1967-1968)
Board of Directors—1968-

Mr. Sanderson was born in Aurora, Illinois, in 1921. He was graduated from Duke University in 1942. Before joining the Chicago office of the firm in 1948, he spent over three years in the Navy and one year at Northwestern University. He was promoted to manager in 1952, transferred to Milwaukee in 1955, and was admitted to the partnership in 1957. He was Managing Partner of the Milwaukee office from 1961 until 1972 and has been a Country Managing Partner—United States since 1970.

W. D. SPRAGUE——————————
Advisory Group—1956-1959
(Vice Chairman—1957-1958
Chairman—1958-1959)

Mr. Sprague was born in Springfield, Ohio, on August 24, 1913. He was graduated from the University of Wisconsin. He joined the firm in 1935 in New York, spent ten years in the Houston office and returned to New York in 1947. He became a manager in 1941, a partner in 1950, and was partner in charge of the New York office from 1962 to 1966. He retired from the firm in 1973.

G. E. STANTON
Board of Directors—1973-

Mr. Stanton was born in 1922 in Merrill, Wisconsin. He was graduated from the Univerisity of Notre Dame in 1947, after serving in the Army from 1943 to 1946. He attended the Wharton Graduate School of the University of Pennsylvania and joined the Washington office of the firm in 1947. He was made a manager in 1952, transferred to the Chicago office in 1956 and became a partner in 1958. He was appointed Director of Merger Practice in 1963, and Vice Chairman—Administration in 1970.

THOMAS G. S. SUMNER
Advisory Group—1966-1968
Board of Directors—1968-1971

Mr. Sumner was born in São Paulo, Brazil in 1926. He was employed in 1942 by McAuliffe, Turquand, Youngs & Co. and joined Arthur Andersen & Co. in 1957 when that practice was acquired. He became a partner in 1961, and is now Managing Partner of the São Paulo office, as well as Country Managing Partner—Argentina and Brazil.

NORMAN TUCKER
Advisory Group—1967-1968

Mr. Tucker was born in Jefferson, Iowa. He attended the University of Iowa, joining the firm in 1948, after graduation. He has been with the firm since that time, except for a one-year interval with the United States Treasury Department. Mr. Tucker became a manager in 1953, and a partner in 1958. He spent nineteen years in the manufacturing audit division of the Chicago office, the last nine as partner in charge of that division. In 1972, he was appointed Director of Accounting and Auditing Practice in the Chicago office. In August, 1973, he became Audit Practice Director for Europe and South Africa, and is headquartered in the London office.

NICOLÁS URQUIZA
Advisory Group—1961-1964

Sr. Urquiza was born in Querétaro, México in 1921. He was graduated from the University of México in 1946. Sr. Urquiza was employed by the México City office in 1946, became a manager in 1950, and a partner in 1959. He was in charge of the tax department of the México City office from 1954 through 1972. He is presently Tax Practice Director for México and Central America.

GEORGE WAGNER

(Deceased—November 20, 1964)
Advisory Group—1947-1960
(Chairman—1956-1957)

Mr. Wagner was a native New Yorker, born in Brooklyn on October 12, 1904. He received his public school education in New York and was graduated from New York University in 1925. The following year he joined the New York office of Arthur Andersen & Co. He was admitted to partnership in 1937 and became Managing Partner of the New York office in 1950. In 1962, he became an advisory partner.

JOHN M. WATERS

Advisory Group—1957-1960

Mr. Waters was born in Hayward, Wisconsin, in 1913. He was employed by the Chicago office on July 16, 1934, upon his graduation from the University of Wisconsin. He became a manager on July 1, 1941, and a partner in 1951. He was transferred to Omaha in 1951 as Managing Partner and returned to Chicago in 1960. He is now Treasurer of the firm. He served in the United States Navy during the second World War, attaining the rank of lieutenant commander.

E. L. WEHNER

Advisory Group—1965-1968
Board of Directors—1972-

Mr. Wehner was born in 1920 and reared in Texas. Upon graduation from Texas A. & M. University in 1941, he served five years in the Army. He joined the firm in Houston in 1946, became a manager in 1950 and a partner in 1955, and is presently Managing Partner of the Houston office.

LELSIE T. WELSH, JR.

Advisory Group—1956-1958

Mr. Welsh was born November 29, 1922 and was graduated from the University of Illinois. He joined the staff of our Chicago office in 1944, became a manager in July, 1948, and was admitted to partnership July, 1954. In September, 1961, he became audit partner in charge of the manufacturing division of the Chicago office with firm-wide responsibility for the coordination of activities relating to mergers, sales and acquisitions of companies. He resigned from the firm October 31, 1963.

GENERAL INDEX